Raised On The Titanic

To Margaret and Peter
Best Wishes
David Haisman

Acknowledgements

To my dear wife Lyn for her unfailing patience throughout;
and for David, Andrew, Janina and Janette

Raised On The Titanic
An autobiography

•

David Haisman

Boolarong Press

First published in 2002 by
Boolarong Press
PO Box 308
Moorooka Qld 4105

National Library of Australia
Cataloguing-in-Publication entry:
Haisman, David, 1938-.
Raised on the Titanic : an autobiography.

ISBN 0 646 33265 1

Haisman, David, 138-. I. Title.

920

Author's disc conversion to 11½ on 14 point Minion
by Frank Povah at The Busy Boordy, Dunalley.

Printed and bound by Watson Ferguson & Co., Brisbane.

*All photos are from the Haisman collection unless otherwise stated,
the remainder being over 50 years old.*

About the Author

THIS IS DAVID HAISMAN'S second book. His first, titled *I'll See You In New York* was about his mother's experiences on the ill fated *Titanic*. At the time of the sinking in 1912 she was almost 16 years of age and in 1997, at 100 years of age, she became the world's oldest living survivor of the Titanic disaster.

Being her youngest son, David has been brought up with this story, and at the age of 16, joined the Merchant Navy and himself has served on the great White Star Liners crossing the North Atlantic. Much of his work on these ships involved the duties as Lookout Man, looking out for icebergs much the same as in *Titanic's* day.

His sailing on those great liners during those very same conditions gives his story greater credibility with his first hand experience, more so than some other writers on the subject.

Although his own life story reveals some interesting facts about the *Titanic*, it also gives an insight to the kind of mother he had and the respect he held for his father. This story however, is not so much about that tragedy but more so about his interesting life travelling the world for most of that time and the many situations he had found himself in.

The author now lives back in his native Southampton with his wife Lyn, and enjoys painting as a hobby.

Contents

Introduction

AT THE AGE OF FIVE, I was on my way to South Africa, via St Helena on a troop-ship with my mother, three brothers, two sisters, and 500 troops after leaving war torn England in 1943. We were being shadowed by a German U Boat for several days during that voyage and it all could have ended there, but luck was on our side and we safely reached St. Helena and later, Cape Town. During the five years of our stay in Simonstown, a small township some 20 miles from Cape Town, I was to learn that my mother was someone special and the name *Titanic* had something to do with that. By the age of ten we were on our way back to Southampton in England and on arrival, saw that the town had been heavily bombed throughout the war. This left Southampton with a critical housing shortage and as a result, we ended up living in a Nissen hut for two years, a tunnel shaped structure with a corrugated iron roof and creaky floorboards.

By the age of sixteen I was doing my first trip to sea, bound for West Africa on an old cargo ship that had been captured from the Germans and had been converted into a banana boat. By the time I had reached the age of 20, I had served on 15 different ships, including cargo ships, tankers and some of the world's largest liners. During that time I had lots of laughs and had endured some hair raising moments with incidents in Costa Rica, Cape Town, Los Angeles and Singapore, to name but a few. By the age of 30, there had been tragedy as well as excitement and it wasn't going to end there. The discovery of the wreck of the *Titanic* was to turn my mother into a celebrity and later, have an unexpected impact on my life as well. Having lived in three countries and visited many more, it became a crowded life but more of that later as I go back to where it all began.

Author's paintings of the TITANIC.

Chapter One
Early Days

Spring Road is quite a long winding road with mostly detached houses on either side as it finally slopes down to a steep hill at its very end. At the bottom of the hill there is a railway viaduct, which crosses the road and a large pond to one side known as Millers Pond. This suburb of Southampton, known as Sholing , was typically English with its layout of three bed roomed detached houses looking much the same. With their bay windows, arched front door entrances, red brick fronts and white upper rendering towards the apex, it gave one the impression of a well designed, family home. They had good size front gardens, usually enclosed with a hedge or wooden fence and a large garden at the back, which was ideal for those with big families.

Half way up the hill from Miller's Pond was No. 275, the house where I was born on April 28, 1938. I was the youngest son of a large family of eight boys and two girls and although considered a big family these days, it was considered quite normal then. Looking back I don't think I would have preferred it any other way as I have always enjoyed being part of a large family. Being the youngest of such a large brood had its advantages whereas, one may well study the elders and learn from them.

Looking back on all those members in my family, I suppose my mother was my real hero. She was a small woman, only about 5' 5" in height, about 112 lbs in weight with fair hair and blue eyes and it was said that as a child, she was considered to be slightly under weight. She was however, very fit and even in her 80's, was still able to bend right over forward and touch her toes without bending her knees. She had never smoked but once in a while, did enjoy a glass of sherry although her main passion was for confectionery.

Her background and upbringing was far removed from the life that she had finally chosen when she first met and married my father. She was born in the Masonic Hotel in Worcester, Cape Province in 1896, the eldest daughter in the second marriage of a wealthy hotelier, a one Thomas Brown, from Blackheath in

London. Her mother came from a wealthy Afrikaans family who owned farms and dairies in the Durban and Durbanville areas. It all meant that my mother would want for nothing and her parents would ensure that she would ultimately, one day become a lady. However, at the age of fifteen, a voyage on the ill-fated *Titanic* was to change all of that and fate would map out an entirely different life for her. This once frail child was to eventually have ten children, travel the world and finally in 1997, at the age of 100 years of age, become the worlds oldest living survivor of the *Titanic* disaster. If her parents could have been around to witness the path her life had taken, they would never have believed it.

After my mother passed away in 1997, I decided that those hundred years of her life should be recorded and set about writing her life story titled, ' I'll see you in New York' Those were the very last words her father had said to her and her mother, as they were lowered down the side of the Titanic in lifeboat 14, to the icy waters below.

275, Spring Road, the place of my birth.

In 1917, my father met my mother whilst in Johannesburg and six weeks later, they were married and it was to be a marriage that would last for over 60 years. Throughout her married life, my mother had always shown unfailing loyalty to my father who always had my respect, and of whom I considered to be quite a clever man that had never reached his full potential throughout his life. He was a man of average height and weight, slightly balding and what hair he had, was of a mousy color, and as far as I remember, always wore glasses. He had spent his whole working life as an engineering draughtsman and in his spare time a keen clubman, being Secretary and Chairman in various political and non- political clubs.

My brothers and sisters. Back row (left to right): Leo, Geoff, Ken, Joy. Centre, at right: John.
Front row (left to right): Donald, Me (the author), Brian, Dorothy. family pet Nip in foreground. Fred, the eldest brother, was away at sea.

My father was a man with a dry sense of humour and appeared to be able to converse on practically any subject, along with a wonderful memory regarding dates and times of important world events. His own father was a blacksmith by trade and was involved with cycle manufacturing and was a close associate of Dan Rudge and Thomas Humber, well known cycle manufacturers at that time. It was also claimed that Fred Haisman senior, was one of the pioneers in the manufacture of the 'bone shaker' and velocopede. He was also responsible for the

' medium height ' ordinary bicycle, of which gradually led up to the safety bicycle. This machine was tested by the British War Office in 1887 and consequently, a large order was placed by them.

His father then began exhibiting machines at Crystal Palace in 1886, and in Paris in 1889 before putting the first modern cycle frame for sale on the open market. He later sailed to South Africa in 1900 and due to his knowledge of safety bicycles was of considerable value to the British Military command there and was given charge of the Cape Colony Cycle Corps. He was publicly thanked by the then, Prince of Wales, the late King Edward the 7th.

At home, most of the discipline was carried out by our mother, who wouldn't hesitate to 'wallop'us, with what ever came to hand if we deserved it. She was also strict on table manners and made sure that we used every piece of cutlery on the table in the way it was meant for. This was clearly a reflection on her own up bringing and failure to observe those basic rules, would end up with the offender receiving a rap across the knuckles, with the ever present wooden spoon kept at her side for that purpose

Looking back, it was clear that our parents had done their best in raising all of us kids and although we were forever getting into all kinds of mischief, we always managed to keep out of any really serious trouble. At the time of my birth, three of my eldest brothers, Fred Junior, Ken and Geoff were serving in the Royal Navy and the fourth Leo, was serving in the Merchant Navy on a ship called the *Aquitania* which was similar in appearance to the *Titanic*. At that time, my mother was more worried about Leo than her other three sons, never forgetting how all the Bell- Boys on the *Titanic* had drowned after the ship had struck an iceberg back in 1912. Naturally, things had changed since then with many lessons having been learned, but my mother apparently would have none of it, and warned him to make sure he knew where his lifeboat was situated.

My two sisters, Joy and Dorothy were named appropriately when Joy, the eldest, finally arrived after the birth of four boys. My mother had been desperately hoping for a girl and decided that the birth of a girl was a joyous occasion. Dorothy, being the seventh child born, was named after my mother's sister, who sadly died from diphtheria back in 1908 at the age of eight. My other two brothers, John and Donald, were numbers six and eight in the line up, and Brian, at number nine was the next brother up from me, being two years older.

I was far too young to remember much about Spring Road but had heard many stories from the older members of my family about many of their antics at

Millers Pond. It appeared that they were forever falling in and arriving back home soaking wet, covered in mud, and stinking to high heaven. There were, knocks on the door from kids asking if they could dry out before going home for fear of their parents getting a strap to them. Geoff, my third eldest brother, almost gave my mother a near heart attack when she let him have an old sheet, thinking he was going to make a tent out in the garden. About half an hour later, there were excited neighbours at the front of the house, shouting out to our

Railway viaduct at the bottom of Spring Road

mother that Geoff was going to jump off of the railway viaduct with his home made parachute.

My mother, in a state of near panic, rushed out of the house and tore down the road in her stocking feet with half the neighbourhood running down behind her. She arrived underneath one of the arches of the viaduct, just as a group of kids already there, were cheering and urging him on to jump. Geoff, standing poised on top of the parapet, his chest, criss - crossed with bits of rope and the sheet fluttering behind him in a stiff breeze, was ready to become the first skydiver in the neighbourhood. Looking down at the road some 50 feet below, he noticed the crowd gathering and his mother waving and shouting frantically up at him to come down. This caused him to put a hold on his countdown and after noticing some of the adults clambering up the embankment towards him, decided to abort the mission. His proposed leap to fame had come to a swift end and had he succeeded, he no doubt would have been a candidate for the undertaker.

I was between three and four years old when admitted to hospital for a hernia operation and although quite naturally I can't remember much about that, I still have faint recollections of standing up in a cot surrounded by white coats and howling my head off. Several days later I am told, I was discharged from hospital and wheeled across Southampton in a pushchair by my brother Leo, during an air raid. Hospitals were becoming targets by the Luftwaffe and it was decided to get patients home if at all possible when air raids were imminent.

The hospital had already been bombed when my other brother Brian, was in there undergoing his own hernia operation. At that time his bed was covered in broken glass and the boy was left shell shocked, never really recovering from that ordeal throughout the remainder of his short life.

After war had been declared in September of 1939, Southampton became a regular target for German bombers, especially at night. My father was assigned as an Air Raid Warden for our specific area and most nights he would be out ensuring that blackout regulations were strictly adhered to. I have seen a photo of him in his blue serge uniform with a haversack over his shoulder and a helmet with the letters '' A.R.P.'' written across the front. He had a white plaited lanyard over his shoulder with a whistle on the end, which was tucked away in his top pocket.

In January 1940, rationing had started, mainly with dairy products and sugar although later on, many more items were added to the list. Throughout 1940 and 1941 Britain was blitzed by the Luftwaffe with extensive bombing over Coventry, London and Southampton along with many other important cities. Churchill had taken over from Chamberlain as Prime Minister as the Battle of Britain got under way. The Atlantic Charter in September of 1941 saw the Americans move one step closer to becoming involved in the conflict. In December of 1941, after the bombing of Pearl Harbour by the Japanese, America became fully involved in the war. I was told that during this time, my eldest sister Joy, became stricken with polio and was sent to a hospital in Alton in Hampshire to undergo treatment in an ' Iron lung '.

With my elder brothers away fighting the war and Southampton being heavily bombed, it must have been a worrying time for my parents in those days. People were facing an unknown future with regular bombing raids on their homes when at the same time, many of their family members were away on battle fronts throughout Europe and elsewhere.

Whilst living in Spring Road, the railway at the bottom of the road received a direct hit one night during an air raid and as a result, blew all the windows out of most houses in the neighbourhood. I don't remember too much about this but was told by my brothers and sisters that our mother had calmly settled us all down again before setting about the task of clearing up all the broken glass and mess. What I do remember however, during our stay in Spring Road were the 'Mickey Mouse' gas masks that were designed for children, although I still wasn't happy when it was put over my head. One of the safeguards during air raids, was to bed the children down under a table downstairs somewhere, as falling plaster and masonry was a danger when the area came under bombing attacks. Not everyone had the luxury of an Anderson Air Raid Shelter dug into their back gardens so this was probably the next best thing other than taking risks leaving the house.

It was becoming dangerous living in Southampton so it was suggested that the children be evacuated to outlying country districts for their own safety, which would have meant our parents being separated from us for long periods at a time. They weren't happy about that so it was arranged to completely leave Southampton and settle in a village called West Wittering near Chichester. This was a small village with a resident population of about 50 several farm animals and a pub called ' The Old House At Home'. We owned a cafe there called 'The Cherries Cafe ' which we bought after the sale of our home in Southampton. Not far away was a camp of Canadian troops who's custom kept the place going and from what I gather, without them, trade would have been virtually none existent. However, the idea behind the move was primarily for safety reasons as life in that part of Sussex was relatively peaceful. The whole village was surrounded by farmland and just down the lane from our cafe was a beach which we visited quite regularly as I remember. In many respects we were quite fortunate to live in this place, and to have our father at home working in Portsmouth Dockyard. To not have him serving in the armed forces overseas, meant we were luckier than most families.

The few memories that I have of West Wittering include the several attempts made by my mother to get me to attend school, and my futile efforts in trying to keep away from the place. There were many tears when I was literally dragged there on some occasions and that reluctance, unfortunately remained with me throughout my school going days. Another memory I have in those days was being made to wear a sky blue coat with big black buttons, the sort of coat worn by Pinocchio or some other such puppet. God knows where my mother got it from but I hated it with a passion and would throw a tantrum every time I was made to wear it. Even at that tender age, I had a feeling that it would have looked better on a girl. Sometimes with a bit of bribery and sometimes with a slap, whichever way it went, mother was always the winner and I always ended up wearing the infernal thing. Times were hard in those days and if something fitted then you wore it and what you looked like, became only a secondary consideration.

In 1943,my father received a posting abroad to Simonstown in South Africa and it was arranged by the Admiralty, that the family would follow him out there at a later date. This must have been a break for all concerned and quite understandably, my mother was thrilled to know that she would be going back to her beloved South Africa and getting us children away from the war in England. My father sailed from Liverpool on a French ship which we learned later, turned out to be a floating disaster with crew trouble, breakdowns and finally running aground in Cape Town six weeks later. My mother was hoping that we would all be going out to rejoin him in Simonstown within the next few months, but it wasn't to be. It turned out to be a long wait of over a year and in that time things didn't go as well as she would have hoped. It was many years later, when we were old enough to appreciate the circumstances, that we realized just how much worry and anguish she must have gone through. There were long periods of not receiving any mail from the four eldest brothers away at sea as war raged on, and being separated from her husband for the first time in 26 years, was of no comfort to her either. During that period, Geoff, the third eldest, arrived home on survivor's leave after being bombed and torpedoed at sea and was temporarily in a bit of a state as a result of that. Leo, the fourth eldest was in Russian convoys and that in itself, was worrying with the merchant navy undergoing heavy losses at that time. It was also during this period that my eldest brother Fred, was reported missing in action and after two long weeks, it was reported that he had escaped from a prisoner of war camp and was safe.

In January of 1944, a letter finally arrived from the Admiralty confirming that arrangements were under way for us to join our father in Simonstown. I was coming up to six years of age and can remember some excitement at that time, as we packed up and prepared for our train journey to Wales. On arrival at Swansea railway station, we were advised to hang on to each other as a great surge of women factory workers rushed to board the train at the end of their shifts. I remember it being very dark once we were clear of the railway station, and that we were being assisted by a police man, carrying my brother, Brian My memories at that time were of us trudging through dark streets in search of lodgings for the night and myself, feeling utterly miserable. After finally finding a place to stay, it turned out to be one of the longest nights I can ever remember, with some of us just never being able to get any sleep at all. It was still dark when we were called to get our things together and join our ship at the docks and after that, I remember little else of that day.

Our ship, the *Empire Grace*, I learned later, was a vessel built by Harland and Wolff of 13 473 tons, capable of a speed of 17 knots and originally built for the Shaw Saville Line for the Australian and New Zealand trade. At the outbreak of war she was commissioned by the British government and altered for troop carrying purposes with accommodation for just a few passengers. We had sailed at daybreak and had gone up through the Irish Sea to Greenock, in order to take on board 500 troops to be disembarked on the island of St Helena, in the South Atlantic.

As we sailed into the Bay of Biscay, I suppose this was the time when the sea began to take on a fascination for me, a fascination that has remained with me throughout my life. I would always try to take a peek over the ship's rail whenever the opportunity presented itself, just to watch the water slipping rapidly along the side of the vessel as it ploughed through the ocean. To get close to the ship's rail was definitely out of bounds, as our mother wouldn't let any of us near it for fear of us disappearing over the side. When arriving up on deck after breakfast each morning, we would be greeted by our convoy of grey ships all around us, noticing that several of them had changed their positions during the night. Sometimes, someone would say something like, ' Look David! That one over there was a long way behind us last night and now she's in front ' or then again something like, ' That one over there seems a long way off today.' and so it went on, every day different to the last. On some days when the sea was rough, I would spend long periods looking out to sea at our escorts all around us, each one in turn, pitching into the heavy seas. On rising up after each wave, they appeared to toss spray all over their forward decks as though to shake off the excess seawater, in preparation for the next plunge.

Early in the voyage, the troops rigged up a swing for us kids on the after deck and this became one of our favourite places to pass away the time. The soldiers were good to us, always having a bit of a laugh and generally enjoying themselves as well, no doubt this being a good time to take their minds off of the tasks that may well lie ahead. I can recall one morning coming up on deck and noticing an empty sea and not a ship in sight and wondered why this could be so. We were to learn later that the convoy had altered course during the night and had headed for the Mediterranean Sea, the War Department deciding, at this point, that our convoy was required elsewhere.

As the *Empire Grace* steamed further into the South Atlantic, I have memories of us sitting up all night, outside of our cabins, fully dressed with life jackets on, the ship being shadowed, by a German submarine. With all those troops onboard, the ship was a valuable target, and as a result, we continued to remain on action stations whilst our ship dropped depth charges throughout the night and the continuing day. Our mother did her best to keep us occupied during that period and years later, we were to realize just how she must have felt, possibly facing another shipwreck, this time with six of her children. Perhaps the only crumb of comfort to her at that time was the knowledge that a soldier had been allocated to each child in case of any emergency

The island of St. Helena is a small island of volcanic origin and just ten miles long. It was under British rule and lies some 1 700 miles NW of Cape Town and was the island that Napoleon was sent to, in exile. The population in 1944 was a little over 4 500 and after our ship had dropped it's anchor in the harbour some three weeks after leaving England, they were about to increase their population by another 500, once the troops had gone ashore for their protection

During our brief stay at St Helena us kids experienced fruit we had never set eyes on before and I well remember eating a banana with the skin on amid laughter from the adults. After the troops had left us, the ship seemed empty and there was a tinge of sadness as many friendships had been made during the voyage. Our ship weighed anchor after only a few hours and then headed for Cape Town, arriving in Table Bay about four days later.

Meeting my father for the first time in over a year, left me not recognizing him at all, and I distinctly remember saying, 'You're not my Dad' as he bent over to give me a bit of a cuddle, a peck on the cheek and then ruffle my hair. Everyone burst out laughing, but looking back, seeing my father for the first time in over a year, was a long time for someone of my age. As for my mother, it must have been a great relief to be reunited with her husband and to know that us children were destined for a better future, now that we were away from the war in England. There was a lot of excitement that day as I recall with the strangeness of our new surroundings and the prospect of a whole new world opening up before us. The train ride from Cape Town to Simonstown was an adventure to us all, travelling on an electric train for the first time and the beautiful sandy beaches and coastline, sweeping past our carriage windows. We would laugh each time the train sounded its horn, as this was reminiscent of an air raid siren when a bombing raid was imminent back in Southampton, but now, a thing of the past.

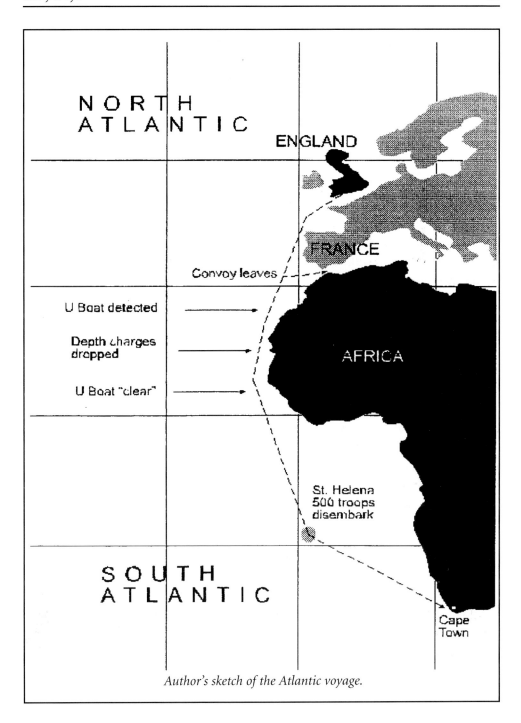

Author's sketch of the Atlantic voyage.

Recent photo's of Simonstown today, still show it as unspoiled and remaining a pretty little township, situated on the side of a mountain, over looking Simons Bay. It was named after Simon van der Stelle, the Dutch governor back in 1679, who also had the town of Stellenbosch named after him which is situated just outside of Cape Town. Living in Simonstown made it hard to believe there was a war going on, life being good for all age groups and us kids getting a good education at our local school. Standards were high at Simonstown Secondary School and our Afrikaans teachers strict with the Afrikaans language being part of the curriculum.

Our first home in Simonstown was named Newry Villa, which was situated on high ground at the top of a hill called Quarry Road, offering a fine view of Simons Bay and the naval dockyard. The road got its name from a quarry, which was further up the mountainside some distance behind the house. This was a happy home for all of us as I remember and it was from here, that us four younger children started our education at Simonstown Secondary School

I can well recall the Principal saying to my mother, as he stood facing her in his study one morning, that standards in the school were high and they would

Residence No. 28, looking towards the mortuary. Note that in this recent photograph the bars have been removed.

turn me into a fine scholar. I can't say that I shared his enthusiasm at that time as I stood alongside of my mother, looking at his huge desk with its ink stained blotting pad, and an array of pens and pencils stacked in a glass beaker. A fleeting glance around the Principal's study revealed two bamboo canes propped up in the corner, one slightly thicker than the other, perhaps for older boys I thought. At the tender age of six I had heard about things such as caning from my elder brothers and I couldn't say that I relished the thought of being on the receiving end of one of those. I quickly averted my gaze from the bamboo's in the corner as the Principal bent down towards me with a smile that fooled no one. With his face just twelve inches away, I took in his enormous untidy grey bushy eyebrows and beneath that tangled mass, his piercing eyes and a whiff of bad breath as he said in a slightly threatening tone, ' I'm sure you'll settle in within a day or two'.

Simonstown Secondary School.

I did settle in within a day or two, just like the man said, and within a few weeks, had made several friends. My recollections of the teachers were that they were all Afrikaners, often bellowing out in Afrikaans with us in turn, hoping to God that we understood what they were saying for fear of receiving a clip around the ear.

The teachers spoke Afrikaans frequently, with no excuses being acceptable as far as they were concerned, if we didn't understand them. After a few slaps about the head from time to time, one picks up the ' lingo ' fairly quickly under those circumstances.

My first school report in June of 1944, showed that I did quite well in arithmetic and was absent six times which on reflection, was a pretty good start for me. My teacher at that time was a huge elderly matronly type of woman with her hair always done up in a bun at the back of her head. She was extremely bow - legged as I remember and we used to say that she would have had great difficulty in stopping a pig in an alleyway. Other features were an enormous bosom and when she leaned over someone's desk to help with a problem, their heads, along with the daylight would disappear between those two great mounds on her chest.

If you had been the one that had endured a close encounter with those enormous breasts during class, then during the break it wouldn't go without comment. In typical schoolboy fashion, there would usually be some kind of wisecrack such as ' I see you've been up amongst the melons again!' or ' Your face was like a beetroot!' followed by laughter all round. Apart from that, 'Old Marj.' as we called her when she was out of earshot, was very patient with all of us, and almost mother like in her approach and we all liked her.

When out of school, there was always much to do, and one such task was learning to swim. My eldest brother taught me to swim, if 'taught' was the correct term, leaving me terrified on many occasions as he would force me to take to the water. He would chase me along Seaforth Beach, shouting behind me ' I'm going to teach you to swim you little bugger even if you drown in the process! ' There were times when I actually thought he meant it. He was as fit as a fiddle and caught me every time despite my screaming and shouting to be left alone, but I just wasn't any match for him.

After catching me, he would wade out into deep water carrying me amidst my protesting and struggling, causing me to be in a state of near panic. He would then wrench my arms from their vice like grip around his neck and throw me in. Slowly he would swim backwards towards the shore, watching me threshing about and at times, becoming completely submerged, as I struggled to keep my head above water. He usually got back to me before I went under for the third or fourth time and would carry me inshore and dump me on the beach. Coughing and spluttering I would shout out words like, ' leave me alone you bloody sod!' the worst swear words I knew at the time, and then in exasperation I would cry out, ' I can learn better on my own!'. He would stand over me laughing and say something like, ' Don't fight it and you'll be fine!' or ' Keep your mouth shut and you won't swallow so much water!' I can't say that any of this was any consolation to me, especially as I thought that I was drowning and fighting for my very life at times. However, learn to swim I did and apart from eventually enjoying it, I also became very good at it as well. As a result, the beach became one of my main interests in life with lots of swimming and messing about in our home-made tin canoes.

These little boats were made from corrugated iron, bent up at both ends and then nailed to a piece of wood at each end to form a bow and a stern. Warm tar was then scraped up from the road and then applied to all the cracks and holes to ensure that the little craft was watertight. For any of our canoes to stay afloat for more than an hour would have been nothing short of a miracle, but that was half the fun. We would race and ram them, always trying to sink one another and when sunk, dive down and make efforts to get the boat ashore, tip all the water out and start all over again. After several hours and quite exhausted by this activity, we would hide our tin canoes in the bushes until next time and then lie in the hot sand, claiming all kinds of victories against each other and laughing and joking about the day's events.

It was around this time that my parents decided that I should visit a dentist in Cape Town to have the remainder of my young teeth removed, although I wasn't to know that at the time. As far as I knew I was just going for a check up and was quite looking forward to the trip. On arrival at Groote Schuur Hospital, my mother was left in a waiting room talking to a white coat as I was led away to a small room further down the corridor. On entering the room, I noticed white tiles half way up the wall, a bed under a window and a huge glass cabinet on one side of the room. Once inside, the nurse loosened my collar and told me to lie on the bed and soon after, went over to join someone in a white coat that had just entered the room. After busying himself in front of the glass cabinet, they both turned and came towards me. My next memories are quite vivid.

As the dentist approached and stood over me with a wad of cotton wool, I suspected something drastic was about to take place but before I could shout out or fight back, he forced the wad down onto my face, causing panic and the feeling of being smothered. As I struggled on the bed, the nurse grabbed my legs and held them down as each breath I drew in caused my strength to falter and then I felt as though I was floating before all things became oblivious as I passed out.

This was the first time in my life that I had ever been to a dentist and also the first time of having the 'privilege' of being chloroformed and in my childlike mind, I felt as though I was being murdered. However, when I regained consciousness from this ordeal, with a mouth full of congealed blood minus eight teeth, I wasn't at all happy and couldn't wait for my mother to get me out of there. This frightening experience remained with me for quite some time afterwards and the mention of the word 'chloroform' would make me cringe every time I heard it.

In 1945, the war ended and although, still a bit young to appreciate the significance of that, I well remember the jubilation just about everywhere and the many parties that followed. For us younger one's, life went on much the same as we continued to do our usual things although we were well aware, that things would be changing for the better. As the study of ships became a real passion of mine, one of my favourite pastimes was to spend hours in Simonstown Dockyard, just walking around and looking at the different warships moored up alongside of the quay. Now the war had ended, the Royal Navy were slowly running down their fleet and many ships like *H.M.S. Norfolk, H.M.S. Birmingham,* and also the *H.M.S. Neiride* and *H.M.S. Actaeon,* were returning to England, leaving the docks looking quite empty.

My attention became more focused on fishing and generally messing around the beaches and now and then, joining in with mountain climbing with my brothers and our friends. One of my constant out of school friends was an Afrikaans boy called Buttie, (pronounced Bootey) who was the youngest son of a wealthy family that had dairy interests around Simonstown. I can't ever remember him going to school but he may have gone to some fee paying school of which his parents being wealthy people, might well have thought would be more suitable for him.

They lived in a huge house in big grounds with many of the rooms at ground level having French Doors. These doors opened onto sprawling lawns offering a beautiful view of Simons Bay before sloping down to a surrounding wall. The whole place immediately gave one the impression of money and Buttie certainly knew where to get some whenever he wanted it. His mother used one of the downstairs rooms as a bedroom and as regular as clockwork, would go for an afternoon nap leaving the French Doors open to take advantage of the sea breezes. After she had dropped off to sleep, Buttie, also as regular as clockwork would crawl on all fours into her room and help himself to the contents of her hand bag, lying on the floor by the side of her bed. He would then creep back out clutching a five or ten pound note and go down to the shops to treat him self to toys, confectionery or whatever else took his fancy.

He would generously treat me, and some of our other friends to some of his ill-gotten gains and at one time, was quite popular with a fair sized following of kids. As this group continued to grow and follow him around from shop to shop, he decided to cut some of them out from his generous handouts for fear of detection. The shop keeper's eyes would bulge when Buttie entered their store, pulling money out of his pockets, which at times, was the equivalent of a good week's wage for some people.

Cutting some of the kids out from his hoard may well have been the beginning of his downfall because although his mother never appeared to miss the money, she must have got to hear about it. Several months went by until one day, shortly after relieving his mother of another hand full of notes his father caught him in the middle of one of his shopping sprees. That was the end of the good times for many of us, with Buttie being grounded for what must have seemed an eternity and his mother sleeping with her handbag under her pillow.

When at school, during the morning break, there would always be some sort of refreshment available for the pupils, usually in the form of grape juice, cocoa, fruit or cheese. Sometimes, other kids would offer their share around if they didn't feel like it and on one occasion, I had eaten far more fruit than I should have before the whistle sounded at the end of the morning break. As we lined up and began to file back into our classrooms, I could hear my stomach rumbling along with the continuing build up of flatulence. I remember this incident only too well as I felt bloated and very uncomfortable, and the last thing I needed was to sit in a classroom for the next two hours.

The teacher taking us for the second period of that morning was a fiery little woman, with a tongue like a lash and all the kids were terrified of her. She was marking homework and would call out a pupil now and then, to explain them selves, usually slapping them across the backs of their legs with a ruler to help them along with their excuses. My discomfort prevailed, as my stomach continued with its orchestrated rumbles and groans when suddenly, I was stricken with fear as I heard that dreaded high pitched yell, ' Haisman! Come out here!' I shakily got up from my chair, stomach churning and colour rising, as I made my way to face the 'firing squad'.

As I walked up and stood alongside of her chair, she pointed at an open page of my exercise book and yelled, ' What do you call this?' Looking down at the blots and smudges all over the place, there wasn't much I could add, other than in a whisper, ' I don't know miss. ' She continued to storm, ' It looks like a spider has crawled out of the ink well and walked all over your work!' She bellowed on, ' What have you got to say for your self?' The brief silence that followed was nerve wracking, as I waited for the ruler across the backs of my legs, which was the usual outcome after these outbursts. My stomach was doing somersaults as I chose to look at the ceiling, hoping for some kind of escape from this onslaught. Suddenly, and completely taken by surprise, she turned in her chair and poked me hard in the stomach with two of her fingers and screamed out, 'Well! Speak up!'

That was the trigger to release the pressure that had been building up in my intestines, and with extremely loud relief, I broke wind. At that instant, my sudden release may well have been heard in all the adjacent classrooms. I felt weak at the knees and wanted to die, the teacher was close to boiling point, the whole class began giggling, fidgeting and lifting their desk tops, as she screamed, ' Get outside and don't come back in until I tell you!. You disgusting boy!'

Sitting outside in the corridor, I felt like the lowest form of life after being ejected from the classroom with my embarrassment now complete.

Fear gripped me as I saw the Principal coming along the corridor towards me, and wondered how I was going to explain this away. Luck was on my side however, as he just glowered at me, probably realizing that if I had been kicked out of her class, I would have been well punished anyway. Later, in the play ground during lunch break, I was quite popular, with many remarks aimed at me such as, ' Changed your pants yet?' and, ' Bet you can't do it again!'

My response would be to give chase, and laugh along with the rest of them, the embarrassment gone, and the funny side of it, now becoming apparent. Looking back on this incident many years later, I became convinced that this teacher must have been a test pilot in a broom factory.

Discipline at the school, was usually carried out by the Principal if it was of a more serious nature and this was a caning across one's backside as the victim was made to bend over his desk. There were other types of discipline carried out by the teachers besides the smacking across the backs of one's legs with rulers or a slap just about anywhere. One of the favourite punishments by one male teacher would be to force a boy up on tiptoe by jerking him up by his side burns. There were times when actual tufts of hair could be seen floating down to the floor when some kids were forced to endure this type of interrogation. If they didn't have side burns he would wrench them up by their ears instead. We accepted this as normal in those days.

Away from the trials and tribulations of school life at that time, home life had it's moments whilst living at Newry Villa in Quarry Road. We were on the occasion, raided by baboons searching for food, scavenging about the place if we were careless enough to leave a window open when we were out. They would enter the house and just about ransack everything and on returning home, you knew that you had had visitors, usually by the dung like smell that they had left behind.

This happened to us during the early days in Simonstown, not really knowing what these animals were capable of and how far they would go in their attempts to get food. We had a large wicker basket out at the back of the house where we used to keep our fruit and vegetables but they soon found that and took the lot one day. At that time we had two little terrier type dogs called Nip and Nap and they would give chase when the baboons were around. We would never encourage this, as baboons can be extremely aggressive and could quite easily kill a dog if provoked

Jubilee Square, Simonstown.

These problems weren't to last however, as we moved just after a year, into an Admiralty house called quite simply, Residence No. 28. This place had bars on all the downstairs windows to safeguard against marauding baboons. It was here that we would remain for the next four years of our stay in South Africa, the house being bigger and a great improvement on Newry Villa. The house was situated at the end of a short upward slope at the end of a cull de sac, lying back on stepped up ground. This higher elevation was supported by a wall of rocks, cemented together with steps to one side, leading up to the front garden. On the right of the steps there was the high side of the building, which was situated towards the front and on the right of the house. This was known as the mortuary, the whole place being once used by the Royal Navy as a shore based sickbay. Directly at the front of the house there was an enclosed glass veranda and entrance, which followed through to the sitting room and dining rooms and then through to the kitchen and pantry. The whole place had walls almost three feet thick and was constructed with material from the same quarry as that of Newry Villa.

All four bedrooms and bathroom were situated upstairs but there were no bars on these windows, probably to prevent the place taking on the appearance of a jail. The back garden had no boundary fence and gently rose up, becoming part of the mountainside and gave a good view of the quarry and beyond. Life in Simonstown for Europeans meant that just about all of them had a house servant, usually a Cape Coloured, as they were known, or a black person. We were no different in that respect, as I believe my father received an allowance for such a service from the Admiralty. We employed several in the first year or so, until finally taking on Josiah, who turned out to be the best of them all, and who remained with us until we returned to England. He had two wives by all accounts who were living 'up country' as they would say, and would send them both money from his seven pounds a month allowance.

'Old Joe' as we knew him, was of slim build, quite tall with a clipped moustache and was of tribal origin. He was a likeable character and had much to put up with from us younger one's from time to time. His accommodation comprised of a one roomed out house with a bed and dressing table, which was clean and quite comfortable. He had all the same meals as us but would never sit down to eat, despite our many efforts to get him to do so, always preferring to stand up and have his meals at the kitchen draining board. My father liked a brandy or two before meals and on Sundays, would give Josiah one or two generous measures before dinner. Sometimes, Josiah would have one too many, and would then lurch about the kitchen, as he bumped into things or broke something when washing up.

When this happened, he would stand dead still with a look of utter surprise on his face, his blood shot eyes wide open, wondering how such a thing could happen before exclaiming, ' Agh! kuk!' which no doubt was a tribal expression for 'Oh! Shit!'

My father thought this was hilarious but my mother, being typically South African, would tell him off for encouraging ' the boy ' to drink. Nevertheless, 'Old Joe' enjoyed his little Sunday 'tipple' with my father, and they were good friends and got along well together. Life at that time continued to be good for everyone and finally, for the first time in 12 years, the whole family managed to get together for a few days. This was made possible by my three elder brothers being posted to Simonstown Naval Base and the fourth eldest brother Leo, serving in the Merchant Navy, able to get a ship to Cape Town.

In 1947, the Royal Family visited South Africa and Simonstown was included in their itinerary. Our School had the whole day planned for us all and we were to wear white shirts or tops and would assemble down at Jubilee Square, waving our little flags. What attracted me to this was a day off from lessons so, I decided to make a job of it and took the whole day off from school instead, and left them to it. I first went down to Dutch Beach, just down the road from our school, and got my tin canoe out of the bushes where it was hidden until I wanted it. I gave it the once over to see if it needed anymore tar around the joins to ensure it being water tight, before putting it back and then made my way into town. The final preparations were under way with flags hanging from balconies and fluttering everywhere from flagpoles and lampposts.

Sailors in white uniforms were lined up on either side of the main street right through the whole town, as crowds began to gather on the pavements on both sides. It was a beautiful sunny day with all the local dignitaries standing in small groups, nervously shuffling around waiting for their big moment. A small naval truck came along, stopping every few moments, to hand out huge 'doorsteps' of corned beef sandwiches to each naval rating as they stood at ease before the Royal Party made their appearance. I remember this event distinctly because as usual I was starving and would have given my right arm for one of those, to what appeared to me at the time, scrumptious enormous sandwiches.

When the motorcade finally came into view, being smaller, I stood in front of everyone else on the pavement. As the car passed by me with the royal visitors, I was no more than six feet away, far closer than anyone that had gone with the school that day as I later found out. However, as they went by, I did my bit and gave Princess Elizabeth a vigorous wave and I'm almost certain she smiled and waved back, anyway, that's my story and I'm sticking to it. After meeting all those that were expected to be met, the Royal Party then moved on to Admiralty House for lunch and thereafter, to Cape Town to join Britain's largest warship, the *H.M.S. Vanguard.*

When I went back to school the next day it was abundantly clear that I had done the right thing by getting away on my own that day. Most of the school party hadn't seen much of any of the goings on, whereas I had had a 'close up', envied by many, when I told them about it.

It was during this year of 1947 that Europe was slowly beginning to recover from the devastation of World War Two with Britain in the grip of one of the worst winters ever recorded. A winter the ' Old country' could well do without with a further tightening of food rationing and many items in the shops returning to wartime measures. There were also problems for the British in Palestine, and in India and on a lighter note, Princess Elizabeth and her Greek fiancé, Prince Phillip, announced they were to marry.

In South Africa at this time I was far too young to understand or even care about such things and at the age of nine, was enjoying life to the full. I was forever out with my friends down the beaches or somewhere half way up the mountainside looking for snakes, baboons or anything else that caught our interest. My other favourite pastime was down on Simonstown Pier fishing, and generally messing about in boats. Most of the boats moored up alongside of the jetty were fishing boats and I could never resist the temptation when no one was about, to hop onboard and have a good look around, poking my nose into everything. On one such occasion I, and a couple of my friends boarded a fishing boat called the *Sea Foam* and I never forgot the experience that followed. There was a small hatchway leading to a rope and tackle locker at the forward end, stinking of a mixture of tar and rotten fish. As usual on these excursions of ours, I would lead the way to see what was down there, the others choosing to remain up on deck. There were only a few steps down on the wooden ladder but having descended to the bottom, I decided that was enough, the smell nauseating.

It was completely dark down there except for a shaft of light beaming down from the half open hatch above me. It was a bit eerie and frightening down in the bowels of this fishing boat so I decided to get out of there as quick as I could. Turning to go back up the ladder, the boys up on deck thought they would have a bit of fun and shut the hatch on me. Quickly reaching the top, I pushed up as hard as I could and shouted out but, as I learned later, the hinged padlock plate had flipped over making it impossible for me to get out on my own. I could hear them laughing as they scampered along the deck above me and clambered up onto the pier, their voices and laughter becoming fainter as they ran along the jetty.

With the hatch now shut, it was pitch black in the locker and with the stark realization that the pier was virtually deserted when we boarded the vessel, the chances were that no one knew where I was except for those two. Thoughts began to race through my mind as I quickly considered the prospect of the pair of them thinking that I could get out on my own and probably went off home. My heart was thumping, as I became panic stricken and began to shout out as loud as my lungs would allow me as I stood at the top of the ladder. I pushed up with the back of my head and shoulders against the hatch with every ounce of strength I could muster but all to no avail, it just wouldn't budge.

My fear had completely taken hold by this time and in this total blackness, between sobs and shouts, I really thought that I would suffocate in that foul stinking air. After what seemed an eternity, I became weak from my cries, screams and the continual thumping on the hatch cover above my head. What must have been almost an hour of enduring this nightmare I felt as though all of my the energy had been drained from me. All of my hair felt wet with perspiration, as beads of sweat from my brow, mingled with the tears on my cheeks, as I despaired about my predicament. Standing at the top of the ladder and stooped over with the back of my head and shoulders still pressing on the hatch cover I thought I would die in this God forsaken hell hole.

By this time I was beginning to feel that I was going to remain down here until the fishermen returned, either today, tomorrow or whenever they chose to put to sea again and the thought of that in itself, didn't help matters much. I descended back down the short ladder and sat on the bottom step completely exhausted by this time and beginning to accept my fate, whatever that may be. I remained hunched over with my head between my legs, at times aware of the water lapping against the side of the boat outside.

For how long I remained like this I never knew until suddenly, I heard a thump from somewhere at the other end of the vessel. Raising my head slightly, the noise was followed by footsteps, which caused my heart to leap as I scrambled back up the short ladder. Mustering up another croaking shout, followed with my now, feeble thumping on the hatch, it was suddenly flung open, the bright sunlight blinding me for an instant. As I recovered my vision and felt the wonderful fresh air entering my lungs with every gasp, I suddenly found renewed energy and shot out of that rope locker like a ' bat out of hell.' I tore along the deck of that boat with my feet hardly touching the woodwork and then, took a leap onto the jetty that would have made any Olympic long jumper proud. Landing on the jetty, I raced away as fast as my legs would carry me, away from that fishing boat from Hell that had held me prisoner and in terror for so long. All I could hear behind me shouting in a strong Afrikaans accent was, 'Where you come from man?' and 'Wha' you bin doin' down 'dere man?' I was in no state to hang around to tell him.

For the first part of that night I woke up many times in a cold sweat, trying to rid my mind of that ordeal, before finally falling into an exhausted sleep.

When I look back at these incidents with the dentist and then on the fishing boat, I have to smile about it, thinking how insignificant it all is to an older person and how one tends to see it in a different light. However, to a nine year old these were life- threatening experiences and had left their mark on me for a very long time afterwards, feeling quite claustrophobic on several occasions when in enclosed spaces. Whether those experiences of feeling as though you are being suffocated by a dentist or shut away in pitch black surroundings have anything to do with it, I really don't know but these incidents have remained locked away in my memory ever since.

The next day at school that pair of urchins knew all about it when I got hold of them and once again, I was told off for fighting, but I reckon I had good reason.

Simonstown pier was the place where I had spent many pleasant hours despite the ordeal with the fishing boat and one or two mishaps like falling in the water a few times. There was the occasion when I dropped off to sleep on the pier one night, causing half the population of Simonstown to be out looking for me. This particular incident came about when my brother, Donald, decided to go out with some friends fishing from a boat and told me to wait for him. He was gone a long time and I was bored and tired so I sat on the bench of the little hut on the end of the pier, choosing a seat facing the sea. Sleep overcame me and I knew nothing else until around midnight when I was woken up with several shouts of ' here he is!' and ' he's O.K.!' Several people began gathering around me as I sat up wondering what all the fuss was about. Apparently, when my brother had returned from his fishing trip, he had looked along the deserted pier and decided that I had gone on home. Until I was discovered, my search party, were beginning to fear the worse knowing how much I loved the water and boats generally. My mother was overcome with relief but this soon turned to anger, scolding me for being so stupid and threatening to ground me indefinitely if I ever went near that pier again.

A hut in the Afrikaans language is called a 'hok ' and my nickname throughout the whole of Simonstown was now 'hokkie ' of which I hated, but was stuck with it anyway.

In South Africa at that time there was a weekly magazine called the 'Outspan' and it was because of an article they ran about my mother, that I first became aware of the importance of the *Titanic* in our lives. It was because of that disaster, that our family came into being and for a popular magazine to write about our mother made me feel quite proud of her. The name *Titanic* had cropped up many times during my younger years and the stories mother had told us were always in great demand at bedtime. I had always thought that it was our very own family story and never gave it much credence as a story that would create any publicity outside of the home. I think the rest of us thought that way as well and perhaps it was the main reason why we, as a family, spoke little about our mother's involvement with the disaster other than when we were drawn into the subject.

When at school the next day, the kids gathered round to hear all about it and if there was anymore that I could tell them. In a town like Simonstown there was never much going on, so this little bit of publicity got around quite a bit and people began to view us differently and wanted to know more, stopping to talk to us in the street. Little were we to know at that time just how much the *Titanic* story would feature in our lives in the years that lay ahead.

I had two good friends out of all those kids I knew and the three of us always got on well together. Robin was an English boy, his family living in Simonstown for the same reasons as our family was and I always remember him by his one shrivelled up ear. Mother Nature hadn't quite finished him off when it came to his ears by all accounts but that imperfect little ear still appeared to function as well as the other one and he missed nothing. He was quite small for his age, fair haired and brainy as I recall although he didn't share my enthusiasm for fishing and swimming. He was a good laugh at school and that really was the bond of our friendship, sharing the same sense of humour.

The other good friend was, Richard, a boy who didn't come across as too brainy at all but always had a permanent grin on a face that was peppered with freckles. He had pronounced 'buck teeth' which would have served him well in gnawing an apple through a picket fence with little effort.

Nothing seemed to wipe that grin off of his face and it got him into all sorts of trouble, especially with the teachers who always thought he was laughing when being punished. He would usually end up being belted twice with the teacher yelling at him, 'do you think its funny? Of course it was far from funny and the ruler across the backs of his legs would hurt like hell but that grin just wouldn't go away. We all felt for poor Richard as we knew that grin of his was costing him dearly, especially when the teachers meant business. One would have thought they would have realized it was just a mannerism of his and

From top: My sister Joy, Nip, Nap and me, aged 7. Richard (right) and me, with dogs. Me aged 9.

should have known that he just couldn't help it, however, it was a laugh to say the least.

On school holidays or Saturday mornings, the three of us would go to the one and only cinema in Simonstown, referred to as the Bioscope, a word commonly used in South Africa. We would watch mostly American films like Flash Gordon, and movies with Roy Rogers and his faithful horse 'Trigger' but our favourite movies were those featuring Laurel and Hardy. At that time, the Walt Disney movie, ' Fantasia ' had hit the screens and we were mesmerized by this wonder of animation on the screen before our very eyes. We would have lumps in our throats, watching Walt Disney's ' Bambi' and struggle to hold back the tears when watching movies like ' Lassie Come Home '

The Bioscope was well known as the ' bug hutch ' locally and when inside, we were segregated, with the black people upstairs on the balcony and whites downstairs in the stalls. Throughout the performances one could witness missiles being flung about the place, hearing the never ending of squeaking seats, giggles and the odd crisp bag being blown up and then exploded. It was a lot of fun and we loved the place, always looking forward to our next visit. Apart from the regular showings of those movies, there were many popular songs heard on the wireless and sometimes in the cinema's, some of which were, ' They Say It's Wonderful', ' On A Slow Boat To China' and ' It's Magic. '

Away from the one and only cinema in Simonstown, you could find yourself walking along the only main street in the town and it would be quite normal to see a Great Dane following a sailor or two. This dog for reasons not known, had a fascination for sailors, following them everywhere and was a great favourite throughout the place. It's owner, became fed up with forever looking for the animal and eventually let the navy have it for a mascot. He was signed up and became Able Seaman Nuisance, had an allowance set aside by the navy and could be seen stretched out on the floors of pubs and clubs from as far a field as Cape Town. When he died many years later, he was buried with full naval honours at the top of the mountain at a naval barracks called Klava Camp overlooking Simonstown. His grave, which has been well maintained, is still there to this very day, and a visit to Simonstown Museum will show a detailed account of his life in the town.

By 1948 and our family had been in South Africa for nearly five years, and those years had been good for all of us. During that time, my third from eldest brother, Geoff, had married a South African girl and my sister Joy, had married a sailor in the Royal Navy. I was now ten years old and had become an uncle for the first time when my niece Gail was born, making me have quite a grown up feel about it all.

During this time in South Africa, Jan Smuts the Premier, lost his seat to the Nationalist Party after 24 years in office and ultimately, this brought about many changes to that country. We were not to notice those changes however, as the time had finally arrived for the Admiralty to start sending many of their staff from the dock yard back to England now that they were winding down operations at the base. Sometimes over dinner in the evenings I would pick up bits of conversations by my parents talking about returning to England and although there was much I didn't understand, I did get the feeling that my mother was happy where she was and would have preferred to remain in South Africa. For my part, I felt quite excited about going back to England, although I remembered little of it, but it was another adventure and there was that two weeks sea voyage to look forward to. Eventually we had a sailing date for September and my excitement increased as the day of departure drew closer. It was also a great feeling to know that there wouldn't be any more school until God knows when and that itself, kept me in high spirits.

At school I couldn't wait to tell my friends although someone had said ' You wont like it because the Germans have bombed all the houses and you wont have anywhere to live'. As for Robin, always appearing advanced for his years, said with a cheeky grin on his face, ' see you in England'. Apparently his family had also had their marching orders from the Admiralty to return to the U.K. At the end of my last day at school we just said our goodbyes as though we would be seeing each other the next day and just said things like 'see ya later.' That was the end of our friendships of nearly five years together and although we all put on a good front on my leaving, I'm pretty sure we all felt a bit of sadness.

When our family arrived at Simonstown Station in order to take a train to Cape Town to join our ship, I saw Richard just once more before he boarded the school bus outside of the station. There was just the briefest of waves between us along with that fixed grin of his before stepping onto the bus and then he was gone, and the end of another good school friendship as well.

Our ship was the *Pretoria Castle*, a vessel of some 28 000 tons, owned by the Union Castle Line Company and was on her maiden return voyage. On arrival at Cape Town docks I remember my amazement at the size of the ship, having never seen anything like this in Simonstown. As we stood on the quay side before boarding, I couldn't take my eyes away from the great lavender hull, the white superstructure and the one massive black topped red funnel. I remember my eldest brother Fred, explaining to me as he pointed towards the great liner, ' now you know what a big ship looks like David' as he took in my excitement and my eagerness to get onboard.

Those of us travelling that day were my mother, father and five of us children. Those brothers serving in the Royal Navy at Simonstown and Joy, my sister, were there to see us off and it would be a couple of years before we would see any

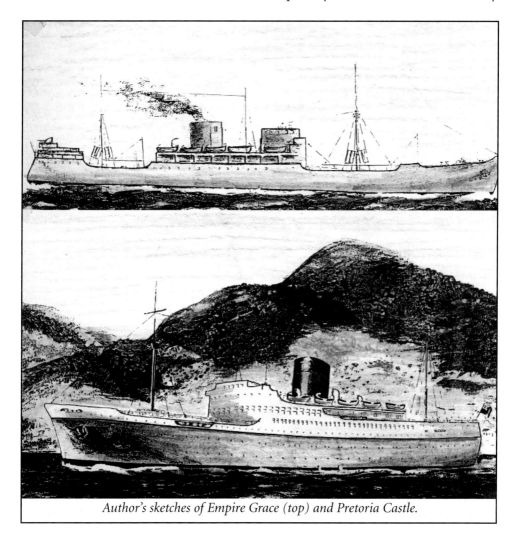

Author's sketches of Empire Grace (top) and Pretoria Castle.

of them again. We sailed at 4 pm and there were crowds on the dockside waving and shouting up to us as we slowly drew away from the quayside. There were many tears that day as a whole way of life was now over. A new future awaited us and it was as well, that we never knew what was in store for us over the next couple of years.

I've always seen life as a lottery,
a lottery that's a miracle indeed.
A lottery with millions of cells involved,
Yet mine was the chosen seed.

The time of my arrival was April,
The year was back in thirty eight.
The last of a very large family,
to arrive on that particular date.

I found the whole process amazing,
to be in on the final selection.
But my parents knew from the beginning,
that they were just seeking perfection.

Haisey

Chapter Two
Southampton

The first few days onboard the *Pretoria Castle* were like a dream to me, exploring the ship from top to bottom, and once again, poking my nose into places where I shouldn't have been. I soon made friends with some of the other kids onboard and we spent a great deal of our time playing deck games and at other times, board games in the ships library. A young girl by the name of Janice who was thirteen years old, 3 years my senior, was quite pretty with fair hair as I remember, and I was developing a bit of a crush on her. She taught me to play chess and I loved every minute of it, gazing at her more so than at the board. I never stood a chance but deserved top marks for persistence, popping up wherever she was, always seeking out her company or trying to get noticed. Her usual response was, 'oh! Its you again, half pint!' or ' you seem to be everywhere on this ship!'

On one occasion, with my imagination going into overdrive, I was demonstrating to her, someone that had just been shot by a sniper at the side of the pool. In mocking fashion of receiving a bullet in the gut, I fell backwards into the swimming pool along with all the noises that would be associated with a victim on the receiving end of such a dastardly act. Not noticing a man floating on his back in the pool, I scored a direct hit on his midriff causing us both to sink almost to the bottom. When the pair of us resurfaced, he was extremely annoyed and spluttered out ' bugger off you little fool!' splashing water in my face followed with several other obscenities. I made a hasty retreat and scrambled out of the pool as quickly as possible as he spluttered and blew water out of his nostrils

This little bit of Hollywood drama that went wrong, had the desired effect, causing Janice who was standing at the side of the pool, to erupt into fits of laughter. When she finally took control of herself again, she said to me between giggles that I was a hopeless case, mentally deficient and should get help. That was fine by me as I had achieved the response I was looking for but, I hadn't heard those words ' mentally deficient ' before and it left me wondering if they were in Afrikaans or English. I had to find out what they meant and later in the day, when I caught up with my brother John, I asked him what was the meaning of being ' mentally deficient ' Hoping she may have said something nice about me, he burst out laughing and said, ' I totally agree with her. You're bloody crackers!'

As the ship approached the Equator, there were deck game competitions and sports for the younger ones. There were eight different events being held for us kids and the first prize was a token for five shillings to be spent in the ship's shop. The reader may find this hard to believe, but I won all eight first prizes and felt like a millionaire. The spectators were laughing and cheering after each event, their cheers getting even louder, each time I went up to collect another prize. I treated my mother and father to something out of the shop onboard, and also made sure that I treated Janice to a chocolate bar or two as we stuffed ourselves silly on all kinds of confectionery that day.

The ' Crossing The Line' ceremony when crossing the Equator, has always been a long standing tradition on naval and passenger ships alike and onboard our ship, it was no exception. The swimming pool area was rigged for the event with a greased up pole across the centre of the pool, the bearded King Neptune was seated on his throne, fully robed with a crown on his head, his trident held in the hand of his outstretched arm, whilst several of his aids stood around him. Scattered around them was an assortment of paints, buckets of frothy sub-stances, stuffed pillows and other gadgets that would be used for the ceremony. Two people would sit facing each other on the greasy pole and try to knock each other off with the stuffed pillows eventually one, or sometimes both, would fall off of the slippery pole into the water amid cheers from the onlookers. King Neptune would instruct his aids to shave the men with masses of frothy ' shaving soap', using huge shaving brushes and a massive replica razor, before dropping them into the pool from a ' ducking chair ' situated on the end of a plank. Women would be painted with various colours of paint, their hair being ' sham-pooed ' in this frothy mess before also being ' dunked ' in the pool to get washed off. It was all good fun and the passengers loved it and in years to come I would witness this event many times over during my sea going career.

Ten days after leaving Cape Town, the island of Madeira became visible on the horizon around day break My father was up and about as usual and called us kids to come up on deck to see this dark purple mountain, rising out of the sea, as it slowly began to appear from out of the early morning haze, still many nautical miles ahead of our ship. After breakfast we went up on deck again to notice that this great mountain that was the island of Madeira, was much closer now, changing its colour to various beautiful shades of blues and greens against a cloudless blue sky. As the morning wore on, and we became much closer, we could see clustered together, the many little white buildings on the shore line until finally, the *Pretoria Castle* slowed down and stopped, dropping its anchor off of Funchal, the capital of the island. Later, when leaning over the ship's rail, we could see that we were surrounded by ' bum boats ' full of all kinds of items for sale by the locals.

There were also swimmers from other boats, diving down into the deep blue water around the ship, retrieving coins that had been thrown over the side from the passengers up on deck. Some of these divers would find their way up to the boat deck and collect money from passengers before performing one of the great attractions of the day. Cramming as much loose change as they could into their mouths and putting any notes given to them, under elastic bands on their wrists, they would then dive from this great height up on the boat deck, down into the water below. Continuing under water, right under the ship, they would resurface on the other side amidst wide applause from the passengers above. Looking back, one begins to realize that this was no mean feat as that class of vessel had a draught of around 26 feet and a beam of around 80 feet at waterline level.

Us children were fascinated by the goings on around the ship with passengers pulling up leather goods, linens and an assortment of items on the ends of lines and then lowering down the money in little canvas bags to the boats below. Our stay at this Portuguese island of Madeira, was only for a few hours before we weighed anchor and headed out to sea once more, bound for England. The voyage from here to Southampton was just a little over four days and my excitement was building up again in anticipation of arriving back to the country of my birth. As the last few days went by, we continued to enjoy our lives onboard the *Pretoria Castle,* having made many friends with passengers and crew alike. The coast line of Cape Finisterre on the north western tip of Spain was pointed out to us before entering the Bay of Biscay and during the next day, we were shown another landfall which we were told was Northern France. Some time after that we would have approached the English Channel and it was well known that Union Castle liners arrived in Southampton each week on Friday mornings in those days. Therefore, it would have been on Thursday evening that we first saw the lights of Southern England twinkling away on the coastline.

Our voyage was now nearing its end and I had enjoyed every moment of it, although a bit sad at the thought of having to leave the ship in the morning. There are certain things that will remain in the memory for the rest of one's life. As a youngster, with a healthy appetite, I could never forget those wonderful food smells coming from the ship's dining saloon at meal times and I eagerly looked forward to every session. These ships also carried large cargo's of fruit from South Africa, especially oranges and the smell of the fruit occasionally wafting about the ship's decks from the cargo holds, was yet another reminder of life onboard the *Pretoria Castle.*

I saw Janice just once more, and that was as she was about to leave the ship in Southampton with her parents as they stood outside of the Pursers Office. I said something to her like, ' I bet you wish you were staying. ' She replied, ' It's been fun but I'm looking forward to going back to school again ' Funny girl I thought. As she turned away to join her parents moving towards the gangway, there was a brief glance in my direction with a half smile, and that was the last I ever saw of her. For a moment I couldn't believe that I would never see her again after enjoying her company so much over the last two weeks but like my friends in Simonstown it was again, the end of another good friendship. My first infatuation with a member of the opposite sex had finally come to an end along with the childhood shipboard romance that never really was, but nevertheless, a little gem that would remain in my memory. This then was the end of the good times and the beginning of an entirely new kind of life for us all, something we were certainly not prepared for.

On leaving the ship that morning, we were met by my brother Leo, his wife and two children and taken to their home which was known as a ' prefab', in Sholing, this being the same suburb of Southampton that I was born in.

These prefabricated homes were meant for a family of five and were designed to help with the shortage of accommodation after the war. There were now eleven of us cramped up in that small home and it was hard going for all concerned. Southampton had received heavy bombing during the war and had a critical housing shortage so any type of accommodation would have to do, until a home became available. Eventually something turned up and we were to finally move out, giving my brother and his wife some long awaited space and freedom again.

Our new home was to be a hut, a Nissen hut in fact, situated in parkland in the middle of Southampton. These dwellings were tunnel shaped structures with a corrugated iron roof and wooden floorboards throughout the building. Inside there were three bedrooms, partitioned off with plywood and a gap of around 18 inches at the top. The living space at the front of the hut had a circular stove designed for coke burning in the centre of the room with the chimney pipe going straight up through the roof. A kitchen was partitioned off in one corner, as was a toilet just inside of the front door. The American forces had abandoned these huts just after the war, and there were hardly any alterations made by the local authority when renting them out to the homeless. If my memory serves me well, there were about 75 of these dwellings, surrounded by an iron check wire fence, about eight feet high, with one side looking out onto the parks and cricket pitch. On the other side of the camp, as it was sometimes known, it was bordered around the edge by a main road.

There was an entrance at one end which showed signs of being gated off at one time when the troops were in residence, and a wide tarmac pathway running right through the middle of the camp to the entrance at the other end. In complete contrast to the way we used to live in South Africa, this then was to be our home for the next two years.

As the youngest, I went to a junior school called Ascupart School, which wasn't far from where we lived and on meeting the Head Mistress, decided once again that I wasn't going to like school much. This was no reflection on the Head however it's just that I could have thought of better things to do other than to attend school.

My first day at Ascupart was an unforgettable experience as once the other kids knew that I had just arrived from South Africa, I became the centre of attention. I was picked on firstly, by the funny way I spoke which of course was in a

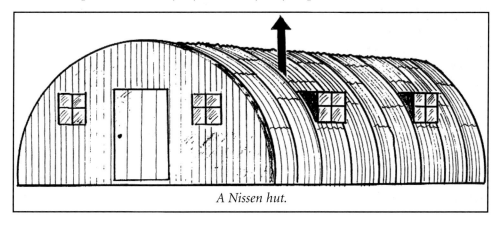

A Nissen hut.

South African accent, and was repeatedly asked to say something in the Afrikaans language. I was also asked several times if I had seen any lions and elephants whilst I was there. During the morning break, and now being referred to as ' the boy from Africa, ' the small group surrounding me wanted to know if I could fight. One of them, stocky built and quite aggressive looking, stood forward and very cockily said, ' do you think you could beat me up?' I replied very diplomatically, ' I don't want to fight anyone. I just want to be friends.' Feeling that he had the upper hand, he stepped forward and pushed me in the chest causing me to take several steps back. I was never one to back down, and in a situation like this, I would usually get an adrenalin rush which in later years, I became all too familiar with.

Before he could take another step in my direction, I leapt forward, grabbing him around the neck in a head lock and fastened onto him like a vice, the momentum causing us both to fall to the ground. I had been successful with this tactic before and knew that I had him, as long as I ' hung' in there. As his face started to first turn red and then blue his voice rasped out, ' I give in! I give in!' The kids standing around in a circle above us were shouting out, 'free fight! Free fight! Which was loud enough for the whole school to hear. After releasing him and standing up, I watched him slowly get to his feet, rubbing his neck as he did so, his colour slowly returning. Regaining his breath, he then spluttered out. ' Right! I'm going to get my gang!' and then tore off across the play ground to a group of kids who had already sensed there was trouble and were making their way over in my direction.

Unknown to me at the time, I had just humiliated and flattened the school bully and it looked like my reward for such an act, was now hurtling towards me in the shape of about fifteen kids, hell bent on pay back time. There was only one thing left to do against such odds and that was to show a clean pair of heals, hop over the school railings and make a dash for freedom. This was just one of the many skirmishes of which I was to encounter over the next year or so, but that's just part of the growing up process that most boys go through and I soon had many friends in and out of school. Years later I met that school bully when I joined an oil tanker and we had a good laugh over that scuffle, with him saying that he thought I was going to kill him at the time. I jokingly replied by saying that I hadn't killed anyone up to then, but you never know your luck! He had turned out to be quite a likeable bloke, both of us becoming good shipmates, but I heard some years later that he had been killed in a car accident.

Life in the huts was an education with a real mixed bag of residents ranging from ordinary decent folk to some real down and outs including the odd prostitute or two. Police were regular visitors to Houndwell Park and knew many of the residents by their first names. I had witnessed fights between adults and terrible rows between neighbours, including two women in a stand up fight, ripping each other's clothes off, to cheers from onlookers. I can remember my father going around to a neighbour's hut one evening in a furious temper, and then after taking his glasses off, punching the fellow square in the face. My Dad must have been at the end of his tether to resort to such a violent act as he never gave the impression that he was ever that kind of a man. This however, had been fermenting for some considerable time and was an indication of how this way of life had its effect on people.

On Saturday mornings during the winter months, there would be a mass exodus of kids and grown ups alike, pushing old prams or anything with wheels on, heading for the gas works in order to pick up sacks of coke for the stoves. This was the cheapest way to get fuel as delivery would always cost more and usually, one good sack full would last until the following Saturday where we would once again all repeat the performance.

Towards the end of the decade and the beginning of the fifties, the rebuilding of Southampton was under way and it was a mammoth task, with a great deal of the High Street having been heavily bombed during the war. One of the major changes to take place was the removal of all the old tramlines, which included those that ran down the Avenue and along the High Street. These tram lines were laid on blocks of wood that were just a bit bigger than a house brick in size and had been well treated with creosote and tar, making them an excellent source of fuel.

As the tram lines were lifted and the 'tar blocks' as we knew them, were being dug up from the road, there would be a never ending stream of adults and kids, wheeling everything they could lay their hands on to cart these precious wooden blocks home. Precious indeed, because in the first place they were free and secondly, it meant not having to go to the gas works to buy coke whilst the lengthy operation of lifting tramlines was going on. These tar blocks were much sought after, causing almost the whole population of those living in the Huts of getting in on the act and their eagerness to get a good supply stored away for the winter months.

One of our favourite venues was the lido in the summer and we would descend on that swimming pool en masse, meeting up with many of our school chums, chasing the girls around the pool and at times, throwing each other in. Some of the kids that never had the entrance money to get in there for a swim, would take a dip in a huge water tank, situated up by the Old Battlements, just off of East Street. This water storage tank belonged to a brewery that was there and was generally understood to be soft water for use in their brewing processes. What the kids got up to in that tank, including immersing their unwashed bodies into the crystal clear water, and swimming around in their underpants was anyone's guess but undoubtedly, it would have given the beer an unmistakable taste all of it's own.

Our other favourite haunts were the few cinemas left standing in the High Street, which included the Classic, Odeon and Forum although the choice was always the Gaiety downtown, especially on Sunday afternoons. This cinema was situated just below the Bargate and almost alongside of Gattis, the Italian restaurant, once known to be one of the caterers chosen to serve onboard of the *Titanic.* After standing in a queue outside of the Gaiety, one or two of the kids would pay to get in and once admitted, would open the back door to let the rest in. This was usually noticeable by the brief opening of the curtains alongside of the screen, followed now and then, by a shaft of light crossing over the faces of those in the stalls. Each time the tell- tale sign of another back door entry revealed itself, usherettes would scurry about with torches, lifting up empty squeaky seats in the vain search of the culprits. I can't ever recall anyone getting caught as by the time the cinema staff had arrived on the scene, the 'backdoor kids' had long since been swallowed up in the darkness.

Kingsland Square, the market place, was always worth a visit for us kids, mainly to ask the barrow boys if they had any ' pecked fruit ' they didn't want. This usually ended up with us picking through a box full of rotten fruit, which they couldn't sell, in an effort to find something edible. We also got into the old Kings theatre which was situated in the Square and of which had received bomb damage and was a 'no go' area. However, we always found a way in and would shoot our catapults and bows and arrows at each other from up on the balcony and other vantage points throughout the theatre. Kingsland Square was a busy place on most days and it wouldn't be long before someone knew we were messing about in the theatre and we would be chased out of the place, always just as we were enjoying ourselves.

During the winter evenings, especially when foggy, there would be the smell of smoke from all of the chimneys around the place and at times it would smell like someone was burning rags or the cat or perhaps both. The stoves apparently were not only used for keeping warm but must have served many of the residents as their own private incinerators. It would be dark around 4 pm at this time of year and for a bit of fun, us kids would go into the park to throw bricks onto the corrugated iron roofs of the huts in order to get the occupants to give chase. When inside the hut as the bricks rained down, it would sound like World War Three had just broken out, causing those inside to rush out in search of the offenders, which was what it was all about in the first place.

As we raced across the parks in the dark with someone in hot pursuit, we would run as fast as our legs would carry us before entering a bombed building and hiding, meanwhile doing our utmost to stifle our laughter. If ever they caught us, which did happen now and then, they would really give us a good hiding, so being a good runner, was the name of the game. One such neighbour, known as a bit of a 'weirdo', was one of our favourite targets, never failing to respond immediately once the first brick had clanged on his tin roof. He always wore Wellington boots day and night and probably slept in them as well and when he gave chase, it was difficult to get a good ' head of steam ' without laughing. You could hear just about every swear word imaginable along with those ' Welly boots ' of his flopping against his legs, somewhere behind you out there in the dark.

These brick raids on the corrugated iron roofs, had happened to all of us at different times so we considered it fair game to join in with the others to get our own back. My parents never knew that I was taking part in this activity but were becoming increasingly aware that I was getting into bad company and threatened to ' ground me ' indefinitely if I didn't buck up my ideas.

There were several people living in this place that were quite expert at breaking into shops at night and then flogging off their stolen goods to anyone that had the money. I remember just a few days before November the 5th, known as Guy Fawkes Night, when a huge consignment of fireworks became 'available' and were going cheap. Those that bought these bangers and rockets etc. hid them all over the place including, stowing them underneath their huts for fear of detection. The police had got wind that someone was ' at it ' yet again, in Houndwell Park and had carried out several enquiries at the camp but as usual, no one knew anything. In those days fireworks were quite powerful as I recall and on one particular night, someone had decided to let someone else's fireworks off before Bonfire Night. Crawling under the hut of the unsuspecting owner's firework hoard, the culprit casually put a match to the touch papers on some rockets and bangers before making a rapid exit.

Soon after, all hell broke loose as rockets, sparks, exploding bangers and huge volumes of blue smoke erupted from underneath the hut which in itself, almost gained lift off and ended up going into orbit. The occupants poured out of the building, swearing, shouting, waving their arms about and threatening to murder the first kid they could lay their hands on. This then was the lead up to Bonfire Night that year, including the lighting of other kids bonfires, bangers being exploded in kids pockets and several of them walking around with singed eyebrows and hair, with home made bandages around one or two burnt fingers.

During the summer months, our money came from taking score during cricket matches at a shilling a time. This entailed marking up the score boards on the opposite side of the pavilion during weekend matches. We would collect our money from the captain of one of the teams and then race across to the 'chippy' and fill ourselves with huge portions of chips wrapped in newspaper. In the winter months, firewood was always in demand and we would sell chopped up timber taken out of bombed buildings which in turn, was a risky business at times, with many of the buildings being in a state of near collapse. We also took up smoking when we could afford it and was able to get someone to buy us a packet of five, which cost around nine pence. After buying our ' fags', several of us would go to one of the many bombed buildings in St Mary's street and puff away on our 'Woodbines' until the butt end's burnt our fingers. We would try to inhale, amidst coughs and splutters, almost turning green at times, but never letting on that it made us feel sick.

Just about everything was rationed in those days and when buying something from a grocer or other, you had to take a ration book with you and the shop keeper would cut out little portions of the book known as 'points' which were allocated to each purchase. I don't remember cigarettes being on ration although several good brands were scarce and were kept under the counter. At school, some sections of these pages from ration books could be bought for several pence and that became a popular little ' earner ' for some kid's. Other pupils at school had fathers serving in the Merchant Navy and as a result, would bring American comics and bubble gum, which was greatly sought after and was also a nice little ' earner ' for them as well. A piece of this pink bubble gum wrapped up in it's tiny square grease proof comic strip would fetch something like two to three pence each and I've known a kid to chew a piece for half a day and then ' flog' it off to his mate for half the price. As long as it still contained some flavour and had the elasticity to blow bubbles it was considered a fairly good deal. Cigarette cards were also sought after and we would swap and deal or buy a wide range of these items at school or outside of the cinema on Saturday mornings.

One morning before going to school, I noticed that all the men folk from the huts were being questioned by the police before being allowed to go on to work. It wasn't long before we heard that a woman had been murdered during the night on a park bench just outside of our perimeter fence. The whole place was crawling with police mainly because of the reputation this place had and of the many unsavoury characters living here. As soon as we heard, we were right there that morning, peering through the wire mesh fence, at the park bench just six feet away, the scene of the crime.

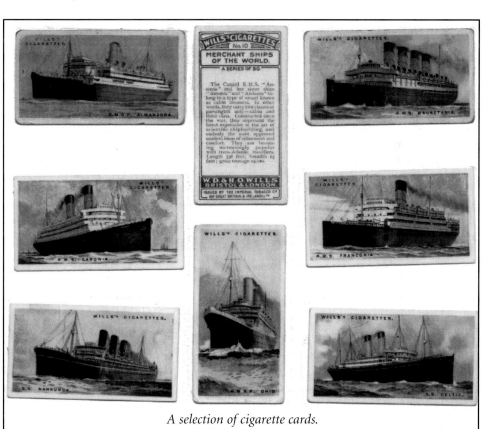

A selection of cigarette cards.

As there had been a heavy dew that night, you could see quite clearly the grass still flattened out all the way out to the centre of the cricket pitch where the poor woman had been dragged. There were many blood stained leaves around the bench and apparently, she had been severely beaten before being moved from this spot. During that very same morning, a man walked into the police station and gave himself up after admitting to the murder. We learned later that the dead woman was a prostitute, well known in the area and it appears, after a long bitter argument with the man in question, he finally beat her up. Realizing he had gone too far, he decided to drag her body out to the centre of the cricket pitch, for fear of it being seen by the footpath. As we continued to look out on to the green, a small black undertaker's van drove up and for the first time in my life, I actually saw a dead body. She was still wearing her red coat and dress although we noticed that her shoes were missing.

Two men in dark coats came out of the small makeshift tent that had been erected over her body, carrying her by her shoulders and feet, and placed her into a long rectangular box lying on the grass. Finally, the men lifted both ends of the box and slid it into the back of the van, closing both doors and thereby ending the drama at Houndwell Park that morning. After it was all over and the area cleared, a crowd of us went around to the park bench where some of the kids picked up bloodstained leaves and put them into matchboxes for souvenirs. Needless to say, these gruesome 'exhibits' soon found their way to school and became the centre of attraction until the teachers found out about it, and quickly confiscated the lot.

During this time, I had left Junior School and was now attending Central Secondary School having failed the scholarship examinations but won a place, in what was known in those days, as a Craft Course. This streaming was designed for children that had good marks during the exams but never quite made it as regards to a pass mark, in other words it was considered as a second chance. I may well have done better if I hadn't been away from school prior to the lead up to the exams but this time it was it was for a good reason as I had been suffering from chicken pox. Central School always reminded me of an institution from the Victorian era and I hated the place with a passion from day one. There were fights almost on a daily basis and canings in the classrooms at such regular intervals that we barely took notice. Some of the senior boys had stand up fights with the teachers in class, and it wasn't unknown for parents to come to school, looking for certain teachers in order to ' punch their lights out'. Many of these older boys had been bombed out of their homes, lost parents in the war or came from broken homes causing the 'devil-may-care' attitude and consequently, were a bit of a handful for the teachers.

In 1950, I had reached 12 years of age and my brother Brian, who was two years older than me, was becoming too much for my mother to cope with. He had never recovered from the bombing as a child and apart from being mentally retarded, and sometimes, incontinent he was also grossly overweight suffering from some kind of glandular disorder. He would at times, fly into a rage and throw anything that came to hand and at other times go missing including going off on bus rides. How he ever achieved this was always a mystery but at the time, it was very worrying for all of us especially our mother who would be at her wits end wondering where he had gotten to. He would be brought home by the police at times and at other times, by a friendly neighbour who had spotted him whilst they were out. His doctor repeatedly advised my mother that he should be taken into care and although she was always against it, she finally agreed. After several months in care, my mother's life became easier and Brian appeared to have settled in well every time we visited him, and my parents beginning to feel that they had done the right thing.

On arriving home from school one lunch time, I was surprised to see my father home from work and my mother sitting in a chair at the dining table, wiping her eyes with a handkerchief. Before I could fathom out what the matter was, my father, never one to mince his words, came straight out with it by saying to me, ' Brian died last night in Coldeast Hospital. You had better not go back to school today.' My memories of that moment were those of feeling numb and disbelief at what I was hearing until finally, allowing it to sink in, I burst into tears and fled into the bedroom we used to share together. It all came flooding back to me as I lay sobbing on my bed, the thought of how close we were despite his handicap, and of the times when I used to make him laugh. When Brian laughed we all laughed as well as it was infectious and would last for ages, causing those around him to join in. This then was my first experience of real grief, realizing that those happy moments with my brother were gone forever. Coupled with this, was the feeling of utter helplessness, knowing that all the words in the world could never ever bring him back. Brian had died from heart failure, which came as a great shock to everyone as he was really looking so well since he had been away from us. It took my mother some time to get over Brian's death but for us younger one's life had to go on and within a short period, we were back with our friends doing the things we had always done.

When out of school, one of my favourite pastimes was going down to the docks to watch the ships arriving and leaving the port, not realizing then, that I would get to know these docks like the back of my hand in the years that lay ahead. I remember seeing the *Aquitania* leaving the port for the last time with her long paying-off pennant flying from her mainmast after over 30 years of service on the North Atlantic route. This ship was a 'four funneler' and very similar in size and design to the ill fated *Titanic* and the first ship my brother Leo had sailed on as a Bell Boy. There were the giant Cunard liners, the *Queen Mary* and *Queen Elizabeth*, arriving or leaving on a weekly basis from their voyages to New York. This was where I liked to be, with my imagination taking over, wondering what it would feel like to be a passenger on these huge vessels or even being a member of the crew on such great liners

At long last, notice came through from the local authority that a new home had been found for us in Bitterne, a suburb of Southampton, relief being felt by everyone. My mother had shed tears in this place and my father had been forever trying to get us out of there, even asking the Admiralty to help if they could. We were going to live in a real house again and for my part, I couldn't wait to change schools and get away from the place. My new school was called Merry Oak and although part of it had been bombed during the war, those buildings left standing were far superior to those of Central School. It's quite extraordinary when one considers the bomb damage done to this school yet the surrounding houses and parkland showed no signs of any bomb damage and appeared virtually untouched. Was the bombing raid an accident or were the Germans really getting to the state where even children were becoming purposeful targets? Perhaps we'll never know however, I can't say that I was too keen on going to school here either, but it did come across as being a bit more civilized.. Unfortunately, I had a bad truancy record and they were on to me, finally catching me out after my sister had written yet another note for me saying I had been ill during another of my prolonged absences from school.

My class teacher, of whom I had no time for, spotted me out on my bike during my 'illness' and on returning to school, sent me to the head master. I had a feeling I was in for it, so I was ready to do a 'runner' by parking my bike propped up alongside of the kerb on the road just outside of the school gates, ready for a quick getaway. Looking back I realise how stupid I was by going to the Head Master's study in the first place, as I knew what was coming and should have made a detour, hopping on my bike and bolting for it. However, on arrival outside of his room, the door was already open and he saw me standing there in anticipation of what was about to happen. Rising from his chair and raising his voice slightly in a threatening tone, he said with emphasis. ' Right Haisman! Your teacher tells me that you've been playing truant again and that's got to stop lad!' I was immediately struck with a piece of simple logic and that was the stark realization that to remain any longer than I had to outside of his study would bring things to a painful conclusion. As he reached into the corner for a cane, I decided that this was as good as opportunity as any to vacate the premises and took off down the corridor like a fart in a blizzard. I raced towards the doors leading to the street, and once outside, leapt onto my bike in a similar fashion to that of a cowboy that had leap-frogged onto his horse in a western movie

I pumped those pedals on that bike for all I was worth but found that after only a few yards of progress, a hand had grabbed the back of my saddle and was virtually pulling me backwards. That old Head Master may have been getting on in years but he was as fit as a fiddle and had me off of that bike in seconds. Dragging me back inside the school, he instructed another teacher to hold me while he gave me six of the best, as they used to say, and that was that for the time being. This didn't mean my truancy days were over, it just meant that I would have to be more careful in future and plan accordingly.

My class teacher at that time, I disliked intensely and I suspected that he knew it as well. My reasons for this dislike were quite simple as his teaching methods were aimed at those that were the brightest and as for the rest of us, we just didn't count. He had his favourites and made no secret of it, which in turn made the other pupils steer well clear of him and his ' clever clique', causing unnecessary divisions in the classroom. His other methods of teaching were humiliating kids in front of the whole class, this in itself a bad tactic if you want anyone's respect. Central School on the other hand, may well have been a dump in my opinion, but teachers there had no favourites as I recall, treating and disciplining everyone in the same way, taking no prisoners.

At the age of 13, I had joined the Army Cadets and this turned out to be a good diversion from my present activities which was forever going up to ' Slab Corner ' at night to meet the local girls and generally fool around as young people do. There was nothing special about this location as it was just a pile of paving slabs that had been left on the corner of the road when the houses were built, and just happened to be a meeting place for us young teenagers. Girls were beginning to feature more in my life now after many of us back in Houndwell Park, had received some basic sex education by a girl known as ' The Camp Bicycle. ' Girls like that never realized what a valuable service they gave to the young male community, giving them a foretaste of what was in store for them in years to come.

I accepted the Army Cadet discipline far easier than that at school and this was probably due to the practicality of all the things we did. Going on manoeuvers wearing full kit with a .303 rifle was good fun and having the responsibility of looking after our uniforms and band instruments made us feel that we were doing something worthwhile. I was a bugler in the band and although I got on quite well with it, blowing it too hard at times would cause my hernia to bulge out, which was a bit disconcerting at times.

Perhaps one of the funniest people I've ever known was ' Froggy,' a boy around the same age as me with a crazy sense of humour. I gave this character his nick- name after 'discovering' him in the woods that surrounded the housing estate where we lived. He had only just recently moved into the area and like the rest of us, was quickly making his presence felt in the neighbourhood and could be sighted at times, scurrying about the woods as though it was his own habitat. He was short with dark hair, fairly well built with a nose like a boxer and resembled a young actor called ' Froggy ' of whom I had seen some years previously in a kid's movie. We became good friends and spent most of our time in the woods building tree camps and various other types of dens along with a good following of kids from the area. There were times when I saw Froggy swinging from tree to tree like an orang-utan, almost as though it was his natural habitat. At times he would fall after misjudging one of his leaps, and with the snapping of branches, twigs and a flurry of leaves, he would land on the ground with a thump. Luckily for him, the earth on the forest floor contained a great deal of leaf mould making his landings comparatively soft and meant he would live for another day. Had the ground been any firmer he probably wouldn't be with us today, but having the nine lives of a cat, he would brush himself off, before scrambling back up the tree, like the anthropoid he resembled. His father was a tobacco salesman, which meant that ' Froggy' would keep us all well supplied with 'Double Ace' cigarettes, puffing away in our secluded hideaway up in the tree canopy. One of our favourite pastimes was the digging of underground camps with built in fireplace and candles all around the earthen walls for our lighting. The whole concept was brought about by just digging a hole about four feet deep and about six feet square with a roof usually constructed from branches, leaves, corrugated iron and finished off with plenty of earth and turf to disguise the whole project on the surface.

As always, no one could leave the candles alone, playing around making little spirals of wax dripping from the burning candles onto the floor of the den. On one occasion, someone decided to inspect the underside of the roof again with a lighted candle and within seconds the whole lot was ablaze. The entrance was only big enough for one to enter or leave at any one time, so it's not too hard to imagine the panic that resulted with six of us trying to squeeze out of that hole all at once. We all eventually made it, although some of us had scorched eyebrows and hair and fell about laughing at our narrow escape. Looking back at the flames that were now belching out of the entrance, and smoke puffing up from the surrounding earth, we considered ourselves lucky that the lot of us weren't barbecued.

Whilst testing the roof on one of our underground camps one day, the whole lot caved in leaving us frantically digging out three other kids that were still inside and were now buried. Within minutes we had them out although one of them had been trapped in the corner with a very hot stove pipe inches away from his face. When we finally dragged him out, he was in a bit of a state with his face looking like he had been on holiday in the West Indies. No one came to any harm that day and the lessons we learned about that little event were not to test the roof by jumping on it when others were inside. Secondly, the one with the face like a lobster, and now terrified of all underground camps, vowed he would never sit too close to the fire next time and probably would stick with tree camps anyhow. When thinking about those underground camps we used to have and the many hours we would spend sitting below ground, puffing away on cigarettes or baking spuds on our stoves, claustrophobia just never entered into it. Yet many years later I would have uneasy feelings about being shut in when travelling on London's underground system or when entering an aircraft and I could never understand why.

Between the housing estate and the woods, there were a couple of overgrown disused tennis courts with a derelict building that was once used as the pavilion and behind that, there was also a deserted old house. The whole complex was ready for demolition and we decided to make use of it before it disappeared so we set up camp in one of the rooms of the house. We had decided that digging all these underground camps was hard work and someone one day was going to end up being buried alive if we didn't watch it, so this run down old house was going to make life easier all round.

There were two old armchairs that had seen better days and also a table and it was here in the sitting room, that we would light a fire in the hearth and bake potatoes or anything else we could sneak out of our homes. To keep the fire going we would rip up a section of floorboards and block up the broken windows with old rags or paper to keep out the draughts. We would stoke the fire until it roared up the chimney and we would stand around it, our faces red from its glow and our mouths and hands blackened from eating half cooked baked spuds with their charred and burnt skins.

There was always one of us who would want to throw more and more wood onto the fire until the whole house felt that it would soon go up in flames but this was the life, especially on those cold frosty days when we were home from school. We felt quite comfortable here although the odd prank now and then would inevitably spell disaster one way or another. One of the kids stood on the table and tried to swing from the light flex hanging from the ceiling resulting in his crashing to the floor and half the ceiling falling down behind him in clouds of dust and falling plaster. Another kid fell down through a gaping hole where a floor board used to be and was left dangling over the basement for quite some time until we finally hauled him back up, at the same time, doing our utmost in trying to control our laughter. It was as well that the whole place would soon be demolished as it was beginning to look as though we had started doing the job ourselves.

Having our den in this old derelict house wasn't to last however as someone had reported us to the police and all twelve of us were summoned to appear before a Magistrates court, along with our parents. After being called into court, each parent had to give the magistrates an outline of their child's behaviour when at home and of course each parent said what wonderful kids we were, never ever getting into any kind of trouble. The magistrates looked us up and down as we stood before them, not really convinced on what they were hearing but none of us had any kind of record so they would have to take us on face value. It soon became our turn to give an account of ourselves and we, each in turn, had to explain our activities when we were in the house. Because of it's derelict state, we told them that the floor boards collapsed unexpectedly under our weight and the ceiling fell down on its own, completely surprising us all when it did. We continued by saying that we only went in there because the doors were open and we had seen other kids playing there as well and we knew the place was going to be pulled down eventually so what was all the fuss about anyway? The magistrates did their best in keeping the session serious and many of the adults in the courtroom that day had a job keeping a straight face but at the time, we couldn't see anything funny and were scared stiff.

Our army cadet captain appeared unexpectedly to speak on our behalf and gave the magistrates glowing reports on our diligence and commitment within the army cadet corps, which we felt really saved the day for all of us. We were all conditionally discharged and had to pay six shillings and sixpence court costs and told to behave ourselves and to keep off of private property in future.

Here I was approaching 14 years of age, well into puberty with the continuing appearance of adolescence spots on my face along with 'peach fuzz' and 'bum fluff' around the jaw line and under the nose. My chances, in the hunt for suitable female company was beginning to look fairly dismal with a face taking on the appearance of the moons surface. There was also the added feeling of embarrassment as I imagined people were forever giving my 'dial' close scrutiny due to the angry collection of roaring red spots scattered about my face. It was during this time that I suffered from the odd boil or two as well and at one time, an enormous blind boil decided to take root on the back of my neck. As the days went by, this lump just grew bigger and became more inflamed, with no apparent sign of it ever developing a head. My thoughts at the time were that it would have to eventually explode, leaving my cranium the size of a peanut.

My father in his wisdom, decided to tackle the problem with an old remedy he knew which comprised of a hot boiled onion, wrapped up in a piece of linen, and strapped around my neck for about ten minutes. As I sat on the kitchen chair with this 'wonderful old fashioned remedy', I felt as though I was melting with perspiration dripping off of my nose and chin. The hot onion was situated right on top of the offending pulsating lump and was literally cooking the infernal thing as I felt the blood and puss trickling down my neck as it seeped out from under the piece of linen. As I sat there in agony, my father was delighted with the result, pointing at my neck and calling out to my mother, 'Look at that Edith! There's nothing like an onion for holding it's heat!' I could vouch for that as my whole neck felt as though it was on fire and when the poultice was finally taken off, I was left with a huge inflamed lump resembling a volcano. At the time I considered the treatment to be worse than the complaint but it certainly did the trick!

There was a lotion on the market in those days that came in a bottle and was obtainable from all chemist shops, claiming that all adolescent spots would disappear within a week or two with regular application. A skin graft would have been more appropriate I thought but nevertheless, condescended to buying the biggest bottle available. This I slapped on with a fury, morning noon and night, peering into the bathroom mirror several times a day, waiting for the magical transformation to take place. Unhappily, the end result after a few weeks was nothing like I had expected with a scaly effect becoming evident and dead skin everywhere taking on the appearance of peeling wallpaper. This meant that going to the local dances with my hormones now in top gear, was definitely out of the question for the time being. Looking like this the 'local talent' would think I had the plague and would no doubt steer well clear of me.

If that wasn't bad enough, the time had come for me to learn how to negotiate a razor around my face and try to get rid of some of this fluff that was taking hold. This operation was carried out one morning when my father was at work and so I decided to have a go with his razor. Covering my face with shaving cream and having gone too mad with the 'frothing up' process, I had a job to see myself in the mirror. I soon realised that there was shaving cream everywhere, over the mirror, on the taps, up my nose and blobs of the stuff on the floor. Peering through this mass of foam, I couldn't help laughing at my reflection in the bathroom mirror, as I resembled something like a snowball with eyes like watermelon seeds.

The art of performing this daily ritual, purely by the reflection in the mirror, takes some getting used to and after nicking myself several times and flicking shaving cream all over the bathroom, I stood back to view myself in the mirror. Not bad I thought, as I decided to finish the job off with a generous helping of Old Spice, slapping it about and nearly shooting through the roof as it came into contact with the carnage on my face. I had watched my father put little bits of tissue paper on the odd cut and decided to follow suit and ended up looking like someone that had just had an argument with a chain saw. Apart from that, there was total satisfaction of having performed another masculine type act and another step towards the eagerly awaited realms of manhood.

In the summer of 1953 and at 15 years of age, our school days had finally come to an end and I can honestly say that I was glad it was all over. My school report showed once again the usual comments,' David could have done better if it wasn't for his poor attendance and frivolity in class ' which really was the overall story of my school days up to this point.

When I showed my parents my testimonial they weren't too pleased, with my father saying that I would have trouble finding a decent job with a report like that. My mother had a bit of faith in me however, suggesting that perhaps my father could try to get me an apprenticeship in his drawing office as a draughtsman. I always did well in art throughout my school going days but I had my sight set eventually, on going away to sea and nothing was going to deter me from that aim.

I was just relieved to be out of school and now hopefully, be out earning my own money, the future not too much to worry about at this time. There was after all conscription, and all of us boys when turning 18 years of age would be going into one of Her Majesty's armed forces whether we liked it or not, as long as we were sound in wind and limb. Apprentices would start their training at the age of 16 and then at the age of 21, once their apprenticeship was completed, would then have to go into the army for two years. This meant that they would have to wait until they were 23 years of age before earning a decent wage which made apprenticeship's unattractive for young men at that time.

On leaving school, 'Froggy' and I, left the army cadets, although some of our mates stayed on and entered the army at 16, making a career of it. The army captain in charge of us at that time was disappointed that so many us of were deciding to go to sea , instead of going into the army, as he considered our training would have been invaluable if we had signed up. However, they still had our support at the 'sixpenny hop', a dance held at the army cadet drill hall every Saturday night, giving us a chance to get amongst the ' local talent. '

The last five years had seen many changes in our lives with all of my family now at work or serving in the armed forces. My father had left the Admiralty at Portsmouth and was employed as a draughtsman with John Thorneycrofts shipyard at Woolston in Southampton. Knowing my great interest in anything to do with ships, he had taken me down to the shipyard to see a launching and also to browse around the model shop. Life at this time had improved greatly for my parents, with all of us now earning our keep and bringing some money in to help with the household budget.

My first job was as a Dock's Messenger with the Outdoor Superintendents Department in Southampton Docks with a weekly wage of two pounds, six shillings and a penny. It's doubtful if you could feed a cat on that today but I was happy to be earning and spending some of my own money at long last. My place of work was the South Western Hotel in Canute Road facing the docks and adjoining the Terminus Railway station. When this hotel was built back in 1867 it was the largest and most prestigious in Southampton with many important people staying there before joining the great White Star Liners prior to sailing to New York.

It was in this hotel that many of *Titanic's* passengers had stayed prior to their joining this fateful ship on April 10, 1912   During the war, the South Western Hotel was taken over by the military and many planned operations were decided in this building by the Chief's of Staff's including Eisenhower and Churchill who stayed here at one stage. After the war, it was taken over by the Docks and Inland Waterways Dept and all the rooms were turned into dock offices, one of these offices, set aside for Dock Messengers. It is interesting to note that today, the building has now been fully restored with much of its exterior and interior being returned to its former glory, and all the rooms being sold off as private apartments.

The South Western Hotel stands in Canute Road, which is named after King Canute, who goes down in history as the king who tried to prevent the tide from advancing on the shore. A pub stands on the site where he was supposed to have performed this act and perhaps, he may well have visited a public house before trying that little trick.

My basic job in the docks, involved delivering and returning paper work to and from all the offices at the shipping berths and sometimes, going onboard a ship to deliver or pick up something or other. The docks were a busy place in those days and it wasn't unknown for ships to lie at anchor in Southampton Water, waiting for a berth to discharge their cargos. When my duties included going to one of the fruit berths, there was usually plenty of fruit to be had for the taking having come from broken crates and boxes during the unloading process from vessels. I would stuff myself silly on grapes, oranges bananas and anything else that took my fancy as I cycled around from one berth to another. Much of this fruit would be written off once the containers had been broken and the bulk of it would end up in the children's hospitals. After a good day down on the fruit berths, I would arrive home after work unable to tackle the evening meal and get a ticking off from my mother for wasting good food.

I can vividly remember another time when I couldn't face my evening meal and it wasn't for eating too much fruit but as a result of being too inquisitive and as a result, feeling quite nauseous after the event. I had been down at the Cross Channel berth one morning when a workmate of mine pointed out to me a car under a green tarpaulin, which had just been off loaded from one of the British Railway's Cross Channel ferries. A family on a driving holiday in France, had apparently been shot dead in their car, by some crazed Frenchman, killing all of them for reasons that were never fully understood. This was the car that had been involved, and had been returned to England by the French police after their enquiries had been concluded. We decided unwisely, to take a peek under the canvas cover and on so doing, poked our heads through the open window. What met our eyes was enough to turn the strongest stomach. There were bullet holes through the seats, congealed blood everywhere, broken windows and what looked like human hair, stuck on the inside of the roof. All of this and an un mistakable stench of death caused us to quickly withdraw our heads and stand back, letting the canvas cover fall back into place as we both looked at each other in a sickening way.

For most people it would have been a distressing sight but for young 15 year olds like us, more so, causing us both to feel quite upset for the rest of that day. That evening when I explained why I wasn't hungry, my mother quite horrified by my story, told me in no uncertain terms that the canvas cover over the car was there for a reason and that I shouldn't have gone near it.

One of the most interesting berths in the Western Docks was Berth 106/7, the berths the Americans used for their troop transports calling in almost on a weekly basis with troops and families either going to or returning from Germany. Other ships that would use these berths and draw a crowd were the emigrant ships like the Shaw Saville Line's *New Australia, Southern Cross,* and *Northern Star* Some P.O vessels on this service included the *Oronsay, Himalaya, Orsova* , and later *Oriana* and *Canberra.* Operators on the emigrant service included Sitmar and Chandris lines as this was the period of the ten pound assisted passage scheme to Australia and literally thousands were leaving these shores almost on a weekly basis. In years to come, unknown to me at that time, I too would be taking part in this great migration down under.

There had been many changes at home and abroad over the last five years with rationing still in force in Britain, but there were signs that it would soon be over. In 1952, the Americans exploded the first hydrogen bomb in the Pacific. Ladies fashions included such things as stiletto heels with many comments in the press about women becoming crippled wearing such footwear. Another favourite were nylon stockings with a black seam at the back, and sometimes, with a butterfly design behind the ankle. Although in great demand in 1953, these items were coming from America and were still scarce, so a bit of smuggling went on with ships on the North Atlantic service. Other imports from America were their movies of course along with most of the popular tunes heard on the airwaves. Songs in the charts were ' Buttons and Bows, ' ' Ghost Riders in the Sky, ' and 'Singing in the Rain '

My employment as a Docks Messenger lasted for a period of about 4 months before I got a job with the Red Funnel Car Ferry Service in October 1953 and at long last I would be working on a ship and becoming a seaman. I was handed a seaman's ration book when taken on, entitling me to double rations of everything, much to the delight of my parents. Being employed as a Deck Boy on the *Balmoral,* the company's flagship, meant that I was on the newest and best ship in the fleet and I felt pretty good about that. Also, the wages were around three times as much as I was getting as a Dock Messenger, although there was a price to pay for such good earnings. We worked extremely long hours, including three nights away from home each week, sleeping onboard overnight in the Isle of Wight. In the summer my working day would be 18 hours long with one day off in nine. In the winter this fell to a 12 hour day and one day off in seven and for all of this, I received a wage of around nine pounds per week This was equivalent to a man's wage in those days and resented by some of the captains as they thought we earned too much money as boys. When the hourly rate is worked out, its easy to see that I was worse off than when I was working as a Dock Messenger, but I was doing something I always wanted to do, and that's all that mattered.

As a Deck Boy you are the lowest form of life on a ship and are at everyone's beck and call, doing all the menial jobs onboard, scrubbing out crew's quarters, washing up, making tea, cleaning brass and washing paintwork You would carry passenger's baggage to the end of the pier when required, run errands for the crew, and then get back to help with the cargo and wash vomit off of the dining saloon windows in readiness for the next trip. This was a daily routine and if you had a bit of time left over, you were made to go on the wheel during the trip and steer for an hour, just to get your hand in, as they would say. The other Deck Boy serving with me on the *Balmoral* was a bloke called Bob, and both him and ' Froggy' became life long friends of mine and to this very day, we still have a beer together when the opportunity presents itself.

' Froggy ' joined the ferryboats about the same time as me although we rarely saw each other as the ship he was serving on, the *Vecta*, was always in port when we were away, and vice versa. When I did see him on the occasion, he always seemed to have a dirty face and scurried about like some poor street urchin out of a Dickens novel. His ship had a coal fire in the galley and knowing what a ' fire bug' he was in the past, his appearance came as no surprise.

The Red Funnel Company had three paddle steamers and I had served on two of these, the *Princess Elizabeth* and the *Bournemouth Queen*. The other, the *Lord Elgin,* was still running cargo to the island after 80 years in service. As one can imagine, these other two ships were getting on in years and the crew accommodation was Victorian with eight bunks in the forecastle and a circular coal stove in the centre for cooking, heating and drying one's clothes. There was a mess room table down the centre and two small portholes on each side. Lighting was by oil lamp and when laying in your bunk, you had the other bloke's feet at your head plus all the noises that eight men make at night when sleeping together in a confined space.

The accommodation was cramped and smelled musty and damp and it was dark down there even during the daytime. Washing facilities were a bucket each, with hot water from the stove if you were the first in line, but being Deck Boys, the men made sure we never got there before them.

Paddle steamers were fast little ships, gaining speed quickly and able to steam along at a good rate of knots. They were also able to pull up alongside of the berth like 'an express train,' the paddles enabling them to do that, never the less they were hard work for all of that. These ships looked as pretty as a picture when spruced up, but had more than their fair share of brass work, and for us boys, it was a never ending job, trying to keep on top of it all.

At 15 years of age, we were quite naive regarding some things in those days and the use of the word, 'condom', never really entered our vocabulary as we always knew these useful little items as ' French Letters ' or ' Johnny Bags. '   Like all young people starting work for the first time, becoming the subject of practical jokes was a regular pastime for the older seaman on the ship. It should therefore come as no surprise that when a crewmember told one of the boys to go ashore and enquire at the chemist about the size of condoms they had in stock, he went without question.

On his arrival back onboard a little later on, and discovering what the errand was all about, he felt as though he wanted to crawl under the first rock he could find until the next decade. Apparently the young female assistant turned bright red and told him to get out of the shop before she called the manager. Thoroughly embarrassed by it all, he told the crew, amidst their laughter, that he couldn't understand why she appeared so upset and why she wouldn't look at him each time he repeated himself. These days of course, no one would bat an eyelid about such things but in the fifties, that kind of talk in front of young women didn't go down too well. A little later on, they got him again by telling him to look for a black light on the night crossing and to report it to the skipper when he had spotted it, but this only took an hour before the ' penny had dropped ', so he was learning.

We got our own back on the occasion, by sewing some of the men's sheets together half way down under the bed covers when they were up on deck working. All hell would break loose later, when turning in for the night and finding they could only pull the sheets up as far as their knees and no further. Another one of our pranks used as pay back, would be to sew up the legs of their trousers when they were asleep, causing them to hop around on one leg in the morning and threatening blue murder if ever they laid their hands on us. Sprinkling pepper on a hot stove when they were asleep was also another way of winding up the crew, causing all hands to bolt out of the fo'c'sle, swearing and cursing as they coughed and spluttered up on deck. Luckily for us they usually saw the funny side of it but there were times when one or two of them looked positively dangerous and would have belted the living daylights out of us if they had ever got hold of us.

During January of 1953, the Princess Victoria, a British Rail car ferry, sank in the Irish Sea with a loss of 128 people. I remember this tragedy quite well because my mother, after reading about the disaster, asked me if I thought the sea life was really something I should pursue.

My father on the other hand, thought the sea life was good for us boys and those sentiments were a reflection on his own boyhood when he also desperately wanted to go to sea, but was forced into an apprenticeship. It was understand-able her mentioning this to me considering her own experience and of course my older brothers at sea during the war years and of how close a couple of them came to being lost at sea.

This conversation took place one evening as we sat in our front room in front of the fire and after listening to my mother, I still maintained that nothing would change my mind on going away to sea. I then asked her about her own feelings when abandoning ship on the *Titanic* and especially, when they knew for certain that things were really serious. She replied with that look of sadness that we had seen so many times before, when she would cast her mind back to that fateful night back in 1912. She went on, ' It was bitterly cold. My father never said a thing as he helped us into the lifeboat.' She continued, ' my mother was very upset you know. She wouldn't let go of my father's arm as he tried to step back away from the boat.' He finally managed to stand well back, never taking his eyes off of us as he continued to gently puff on his cigar.' There was a far away look as she went on, ' I've never seen my father look so sad as he did on that night. He knew what was in store for him and the other gentlemen, as they gathered around on the boat deck that night, watching the women and children being lowered down the ship's side.'

Leaning forward to poke the fire, my mother went on, ' As we were about to be lowered, a man jumped into the boat dressed as a woman and the officer in charge shouted out to him, '' I've got a good mind to shoot you! You could have capsized the boat!" She went on, 'everyone was terribly upset you know. Women and children were crying and my mother was shouting out to my father to find another boat. He just stood there. Never taking his eyes off of us and then as we started to be lowered, he shouted out to us, '' I'll see you in New York!" Reliving it all again for a moment, she went on sadly, ' Those were the last words we were to ever hear from him and as we got further down, we lost sight of each other and never saw him again.' She then said, ' we nearly tipped up when almost reaching the water as one end got stuck as the other continued going down. Everyone was falling all over the place and screaming until we crashed into the water. Freezing cold seawater splashed over all of us and the rest of that night they tried to get rid of the water in the bottom of the boat but it just stayed there. Our boots were soaking wet and our feet were freezing.' She continued, ' My mother was so upset and seeing her like that was very upsetting for me as well.' She finally ended our little chat with something I hadn't heard about up until then by saying, ' My father's brother was a ship's captain you know and he was lost at sea as well.'

I had heard this story before when younger but that evening for some unknown reason, I was beginning to see that disaster for the first time and began to take a greater interest in the subject. It may appear that my mother spoke often about the disaster but that wasn't the case. It was only on the rare occasion when the matter was brought up that we could persuade her to tell us about that tragedy, and usually say something like, ' I'll never understand why all you boys want to go to sea.'

Before qualifying to join the Merchant Navy in those days, the boys would have to go to sea school for six months and basically learn the ropes. Other ways to qualify would be to have some considerable time at sea either on, ocean fishing boats or ferry services such as the company I was with. By the end of 1954, I had more than my qualifying time in, and was now ready to take the plunge and sign on in the Merchant Navy. After seeing the shipping federation doctor, I was told that I wasn't going anywhere until I had my hernia operated on. This was disappointing, as I was so keen to go away to sea but like the man said, it will only get worse as I get older so I had to stay ashore for a few more months to get the job done.

Going to school just got in the way,
Of doing the things that I please.
Like choosing the time to go out and
play,
Building camps and climbing the trees.

I had other plans, although just a kid,
Messing around and playing the fool.
Just pleasing myself whatever I did,
Beat the hell out of going to school.

Haisey.

Chapter Three
Spreading My Wings

At the age of 16, I was of medium height and had a good physique, much of which I put down to all the swimming I did in my earlier years. I also had a mop of blond hair, but not as blond as it was a few years back. I was also considered by some to be a bit of fun to be with and had a wide range of friends. Several girl friends featured in my life up to this point in time, and I was now going steady with a girl by the name of Sandra of whom I didn't really deserve. I would let her down quite often, choosing to go out with my mates, as I didn't want to get into anything too serious just then. After about a year, she decided enough was enough and we finally broke up after she felt that I was never around as much as I should be and realising that once I had gone to sea, it would be even less. After a couple of years at sea and home on leave, I met her again in the street and was staggered by the way she had developed into such a beautiful young woman. This was another lesson to be learned in the growing up cycle, realising that they don't come along like that very often, and I should consider treating them a bit better in future.

Me, Bob and ' Froggy' were getting around to all the local dances and having a lot of fun although ' Froggy ' was beginning to insist that we call him Patrick, especially in front of the opposite sex. This was his proper name after all, and the transition was difficult for a time trying to get used to it, so we used to emphasise the word ' Patrick' just to rub it in. In his usual way he would always laugh it off but Patrick, like the rest of us, was entering into the realms of manhood. In typical fashion to emphasise his point he would do his wonderful impression of the Hunch Back Of Notra Dame by stooping over and turning his face to one side and as he did so, would roll his eyes around in his head. Rubbing his hands together as though washing them, he would say in a rasping voice, which would come out from the corner of his mouth, ' with my face you need all the help you can get!' This wasn't true of course but he could always laugh at himself in any situation.

The times that we were experiencing, were the beginning of the times of our new role as men of the world, and we were witnessing the last remnants of our childhood, disappearing for ever. The three of us were soon to part- company on going away to 'deep sea ' as it was known, and it would be several years before any of us would meet up again.

At long last, the nation could tear up their ration books as rationing had finally ended in July of 1954 and for a while the whole population went mad buying all those things that had been scarce for so long.

Confectionery was the greatest item in demand although I can remember my mother saying to my father that she couldn't believe it, when the grocer asked how much cheese and butter would she like to order with her shopping, that week. In those days, super markets hadn't yet featured in our lives and the house-hold weekly shopping, was usually carried out at the local grocery store by placing an order during the week, and then picking up the groceries on pay day.

I finally joined the Merchant Navy in December 1954, and in January 1955, I walked up the gangway with all my gear, and boarded an Elders and Fyffe's banana boat, the M.V. *Nicoya*, an ex German prize vessel of 2 300 tons. It's said amongst seamen, that a first trip to sea is never forgotten and in my case, I was no exception. On the first day out at sea, the First Mate, a swarthy looking man, called me into the wheel house and said to me in a strong North Country accent, ' when you signed on lad, one of your conditions of employment stated that you should have every Saturday afternoon and all day Sunday off.' My heart jumped a bit as this didn't sound too bad and laying up on deck in the sun on my day off would be just what the ' doctor ordered.' Looking at me as though I had just crawled out of a piece of cheese he went on. ' What the hell you're going to do with a day off onboard here, God only knows!' He then said, almost as a matter of fact. ' Usually, the 'Peggy' has an arrangement with the crew and continues get-ting their grub and generally keeps the mess rooms clean on those days.'

My face must have dropped as I stood there looking at him with the realisa-tion that my time off had just flown out of the wheelhouse window. After picking up a pair of binoculars to look at a ship on the horizon, he turned back to me, and reminding me of a school teacher losing patience with a pupil said, 'Do you understand what I'm saying lad? They'll have a "whip round" and col-lect a "few bob" for you!'

When I got below and put it to the crew, they agreed that I should carry on working throughout the weekend and as one of them said, ' we'll look after you

Pegs.' As a Deck Boy, I was known as the ship's 'Peggy', a very old expression used by seaman, and from this point onwards until I returned home, I would never be called by my proper name again. I had never found out throughout my sea going career, where the word ' Peggy' had originated from, but I'm sure it must have been derived from the days of slave ships. When I found out what my workload was I began to wonder what I was supposed to do for sleep. Apart from cleaning all the accommodation out daily, I was expected to go on deck in the afternoon and clean paintwork and work in the lifeboats. There was the captain's inspection three times a week and all the lockers, tables and chairs were of unvarnished wood and showed every mark. These had to be scrubbed clean until they were almost white and to achieve that, I would have to scrub all the mess room furniture with neat limejuice before washing it off with soapy water. The wide range of detergents available today were never heard of then and if they were, the ship owners would have still preferred you to use elbow grease, being that much cheaper.

Limejuice could always be found on many British Merchantmen, which dates back to the time when it was used to help prevent scurvy. In its neat and concentrated state, the juice is like acid and requires plenty of sugar if ever you chose to drink it. This little 'snippet' of information passed on to me by an old 'sea dog' onboard, came in very useful and saved me a great deal of hard work. It was also this old 'sea dog' that showed me how to unblock a lavatory by rolling up his sleeve and plunging his arm down around the 'S' bend.

One morning, as he carried out this procedure with his arm completely submerged and his head almost inside the pan, he turned his head sideways and said in his broad West Country accent, ' a bit o' shit won't hurt ya lad!' He was right. As long as it was his arm down around the 'S' bend and not mine, it wouldn't hurt at all. With the showers, toilets, and cabins to clean, there were also meals to be collected three times a day, all dished up on plates from the ship's galley. This was situated half way along the vessel at amidships, and from here I would have to struggle along the deck to get right aft in order to put the food on the mess room tables for the crew.

During the early part of the voyage, with heavy seas in the Bay of Biscay, I did my best to keep steady when walking along the heaving deck during one particular mealtime, with three plates of food strung along each arm. Progress was slow, first with a couple of steps forward and then three steps backward, a little stagger sideways and then another attempt to move forward. With one leg up in the air, poised to take another step, the ship buried its head into another huge wave and I lost my balance. I had misjudged the motion and found myself sitting on the deck covered in gravy, meat and three veg, with the dinner plates 'wheeling' around in all directions. Returning to the galley in order to load up once more, the cook wasn't a happy man, yelling at me to watch my step next time or ' the bloody lot of ya can starve!'

On another occasion, the boatswain told me to go and find out what kind of creation the cook had organised for dinner that day. When I arrived outside of the galley, the cook was standing over his hot stove stirring something in a huge pot, red faced with sweat dripping off of his chin and looking quite fearsome. Using the same words as the boatswain, I said sheepishly, ' the boatswain wants to know what creation you've got for us today?' Turning towards me, and reaching boiling point, I thought he was going to throw the ladle at me as he exploded, ' Tell your bloody lot and the boatswain that you've got monkey shit and hailstones followed by Chinese wedding cake, now piss off!' Making a rapid retreat, I found the boatswain up on deck and told him what the cook had said and asked him what he meant. He burst out laughing saying, ' he means curry and rice followed by rice pudding lad!' and then went on, ' don't let that miserable bastard worry you son. It's the heat in the galley that makes 'em like that!'

On arrival at Port Victoria in West Africa, we discharged mail, before proceeding up into the jungle to Tiko, the little native village where we would load our cargo of bananas. We continued slowly up the muddy river, with trees and mangroves along the banks on each side and, a few 'dug out' canoes, keeping pace with us.

The *Nicoya*, on reaching a bend in the river, slowed down further and then purposely, ran her bow into the mud on the riverbank. With her rudder hard over and engines still going ahead, she slowly brought her stern around until facing up stream. From this position she then went astern and gently came up alongside of the loading berth, with her bow now facing down stream she was ready for departure, once loaded.

After three days of loading around 100 000 stems of bananas, we set sail for home and after breaking down more than half a dozen times during the homeward passage, we finally limped into Garston docks in Liverpool. As a result of continuing engine room trouble, a great deal of the cargo had ripened off and was lost regarding to being sold commercially. My pay- off, when leaving the ship came to around 12 pounds sterling and on arrival at Lime Street station, those crew travelling with me, asked how much money I had received from the money that had been collected for my weekend work. I looked at them blankly as we sat in the railway carriage before saying, ' I never got anything.' One of them laughed and said, ' come on Pegs! We won't get you to buy us all a beer. How much did you get?' Again I replied that no one had given me a penny since signing off other than receiving my wages and as it was a collection, I wasn't going to go around and ask for it.

They began to look at each other, realising that I was telling the truth, and knew that the Lamp Trimmer had carried out the collection, and then told everyone onboard that he had paid me. I was led to believe that everyone had put a pound sterling in the 'kitty' each, bringing a total of well over 12 pounds collected by the crew. This meant the Lamp Trimmer had ripped me off for 12 pounds at least, which would have doubled my take home pay, if ever I had received it.

Those few seamen that were sitting with me on that train used about every swear word ever uttered from a man's mouth and threatened to ' beat the hell out of the bastard' if ever they set eyes on him again. When we pulled into Southampton Central Station, those blokes had another 'whip round' on leaving the train, shoving a few notes into my hand as a bit of compensation. This then was the end of my first trip to sea and I thought at the time, that it was as much as I had expected. I had been warned before hand, from some of the seamen on the ferries, what life was going to be like once I had gone away to sea. The great disappointment was the 'low life' of whom could rob a boy and his shipmates but thankfully, this was a 'one off ' as I was never to witness this again throughout my seagoing career.

It felt good to be home again, and to meet up with people of my own age group as I was the only boy onboard the *Nicoya* and felt inferior to just about everyone else on that ship. I had learned a great deal on that voyage regarding shipboard routine, exercising self discipline, along with the expectancy by everyone for you to act like a man at all times.

I was off to the big dances again each week that were held every Saturday night at Southampton's Guild Hall, and always hoping I would be lucky enough to meet a girl to take out or take to the movies. There was much to see at that time with the most popular films being, ' Cat On A Hot Tin Roof ', Blackboard Jungle and 'The Seven Year Itch', starring Marilyn Monroe. Also, the latest craze to hit the cinema's were the 3D films where you sat in the audience wearing red and green glasses to get the three dimensional effect.

Leave entitlement was for a couple of weeks and my money, which was about the equivalent to two weeks pay, would soon run out, so after giving my mother something for my keep, it wasn't long before I was broke. I would now have to find another ship and once signed on, I would be able to take out 'an advance note', this being a sub on wages not yet earned. That way I would have a bit of money for my last few nights ashore, and like most seamen at that time, live it up a bit.

We could pick our ships during those days as there were plenty to choose from in such a busy port as Southampton. I was however, ' Shanghai'd' by a Shipping Federation official, commonly known to the more experienced seafarer as, ' Shanghai Jack,' who was desperate to get a crew together for a Shell oil tanker that would be sailing in February. I was told the ship would be going to Stanlow, up in the Manchester Ship Canal, and then on to Curacao, in Venezuela, and then back to the U.K., the whole round voyage being of just six weeks duration. This sounded fine by me, so I decided to sign on and told my family and friends that I was going to do a ' nice little run' down to South America and would be seeing them all again in about six weeks time. Unknown to me at the time, ' Shanghai Jack' had just ' hooked' another victim and once I had signed the ships running agreement, the Shell Oil Company had my body for the next two years. I left Southampton in February, and never arrived back home again until I had signed off in Hong Kong, and flew back to the U.K. a year and four months later!

To write about this voyage in its entirety, would be to write another book and I have no intention of subjecting the reader to 'overkill' regarding life in the British Merchant Navy in those days. I shall only refer to some of the outstanding aspects of that voyage, in the hope that it may be of interest and give some insight on the way things may have changed over the years.

The Shell tanker, *Niso,* in those 16 months after I joined her, was to take me to four continents, including the Mediterranean, the Middle East and Far East, Singapore, Indonesia, Japan and four months on the Australian coast. Our base was Singapore during the latter part of the voyage and it was from here that we took cargos to Indonesia, Japan and Australia. We arrived on the Australian coast after nine months into our voyage and by that time many crewmembers had decided that they were going no further having had enough and ' jumped ship' at different ports around the coast. It was a far from happy vessel, never knowing where you were going from one week to the next and not having the faintest idea if we would ever pay off before our two year term of 'articles' had expired.

Our first port of call whilst on the Australian coast was Geelong, and after discharging a part cargo, proceeded up to Newcastle and then up through the Great Barrier Reef and onto Townsville and Cairns before returning to Singapore to repeat the process. Watch keeping on deck when serving on cargo ships usually comprises of three seamen and an officer on the bridge during darkness, with one man on the wheel, the other on lookout and the third on standby and relieving the other two. During one of these voyages we encountered an unusual event in the early hours of the morning whilst I was on the twelve to four watch and doing my two hours 'trick' on the wheel.

There was a bit of spray coming over the foc'sle head as the weather had deteriorated slightly and the Lookout phoned the bridge to ask if he could carry on with his lookout duties up on the 'monkey island', this being on top of the wheelhouse. This is normal procedure and the officer of the watch allowed him to do so, as we could just barely see his shape in the darkness through the wheelhouse windows as he came aft along the flying bridge which is the walkway between the foc'sle and bridge housing. As the Lookout Man was about half way along the flying bridge, the ship started to 'climb a hill' or that's what it felt like, as her bow rose ever higher until finally, dropping suddenly and pitching down, burying it's nose into a massive wave. At that stage, the forward part of the ship was completely submerged as a solid wall of water hit our wheelhouse windows. The stern of the vessel had risen so high out of the water that enormous vibration could be heard throughout the vessel as her huge propeller thrashed around in mid air.

Our first concerns were for the Lookout Man but we soon learned that he had made a run for it, sheltering behind the bridge housing as a solid wall of water passed just feet away from him. It was to be his lucky day as just a minute or so sooner, when he was still forward up in the bow, he would have disappeared under that massive wave and would have gone over the side. Immediately after this incident, the sea appeared to settle down again to just a gentle swell but not before the whole ship's crew had been tossed out of their bunks. The captain immediately came up on the bridge in his pyjamas, first looking into the compass and then asking the officer of the watch about the Lookout Man and also if he thought any damage had occurred. Satisfying themselves that we were none the worse for this incident, it was decided between them that we had encountered a freak wave. This phenomenon is a rare event but not unknown throughout the world's oceans and has been thought responsible for the mysterious loss of many ships throughout the ages.

On another occasion whilst on this coast, I was on lookout on the foc'sle head on a beautiful night and on such a night, its quiet up there with just the slight sound of the bow wave breaking away as the vessel steams through the night. Sometimes I would have dolphins to keep me company as they would race towards the bow of the ship, looking very much like torpedoes as the phosphorus lights up their trail. I had seen this many times in my sea career and have always thought of how frightening this must have been to Lookouts on ships during the war. On this particular night however, all was quiet until there was a sudden loud gush of water and air, which nearly brought about an evacuation of the bowels. Rushing to look over the side, I could see that we had just struck a whale and the noise was coming from its blowhole. Its huge tail rose out of the water almost up to where I was standing before crashing back down into the sea, and finally disappearing. We were never to know if the whale had been injured or killed but it's just one of those things that were completely out of our control and one can only hope that the animal was uninjured from it's experience and lived to see another day. Apart from the odd mishap, the coastline was interesting to say the least when looking through binoculars at the scenery, including some of the beaches, mountains and of course sailing through the beautiful Great Barrier Reef.

The *Niso* was an older type vessel with three sharing a cabin, no air conditioning and very little else for crew comfort. The *ship* was a spirit tanker of some 26 000 tons, carrying many different grades of light oils such as kerosene, white spirit, aviation spirit etc., and delivering these cargo's to wherever the demand dictated. Whilst loading in Singapore with several different grades of oils one weekend, we were at the stage in the loading process, where we were at our most dangerous. A ship with tanks partially filled with high flash point liquids, develops a high gas presence, and this is generally known to be one of the most dangerous times for a vessel.

Just ahead of us, a large ship that was approaching a berth just astern of us apparently had complete power failure and the only emergency procedure available at a time like that is to drop both anchors. This was carried out onboard the vessel without delay as we all stood at our ship's rail, watching the impending drama unfolding before our very eyes. The way the ship was headed, left us in no doubt that she would strike our starboard side if the anchors couldn't hold her back. There were efforts to put fenders over the side but vessels of this size need big fenders, which are extremely heavy and cumbersome, and there just wasn't the time anyway. It was normal practice for ships to berth at this terminal without the aid of tugs, which if used, may well have averted the collision that followed. Our Pumpman onboard, realising the immediate danger, had the pumping stopped ashore and ordered us all to shut down as many valves as possible in a futile attempt to lesson the danger, but it was a wasted effort.

The anchors had done little to slow down the approaching vessel and within a minute or so, she struck us just forward of the bridge. The ship was a vessel of some 20 000 tons and on impact, heeled over considerably, making a thunderous roar as she continued to drag anchors, scraping and banging along our ships side, buckling plates, popping rivets, and causing paintwork, rust and sparks to fly everywhere. With huge clouds of brown rust billowing up from between both vessels and the smell of friction still in the air, the ship eventually came to rest further along the quayside. The presence of so much gas wafting around our decks along with volatile liquids 'sloshing' about in the bottoms of our tanks, we

Shell tanker Niso *at Alexandria.*

were a 'bomb' waiting to go off and none of us would have stood a chance if that lot had ignited.

The boatswain, a wiry little man with a crop of ginger curly hair that had never seen a comb in it's life, had stood motionless throughout the whole ordeal, watching the approaching vessel from the ship's rail. Finally, turning towards us and sweeping his arm around in a circular motion, said in his strong Liverpool accent. ' We could have all been on our way to the bloody moon if this lot had gone up!' I think most of us agreed with him on that point as the smell from the petroleum products in our tanks smelled stronger than ever and it was indeed another lucky day for us all..

It was a blessing in disguise for us as the marine surveyors strongly advised the company that the *Niso* should be dry docked immediately for a full survey below the water line. It was also decided that once dry docked, the company would man the ship, this time with a Chinese crew and pay us all off and fly us home. Many Shell tankers were crewed by the Chinese on the Far Eastern trade at that time and we were one of the last to be handed over, so we certainly began to look forward to that.

After dry dock, we set sail for Hong Kong in order for a further refit and for the crew change over. On leaving the ship, we stayed in a Seamen's mission for a few days before flying out of Hong Kong on a B.O.A.C Argonaut which took us just over three days, stopping everywhere to refuel, before we finally arrived in London.

To say it was good to be home was an understatement but at long last that voyage had finally ended and I had quite a bit of leave to come. Having been promoted to an Ordinary Seaman during the voyage and also receiving a pay rise, I had well over a hundred pounds to spend, which was nothing short of a small fortune in those days for a seventeen year old. Many of my friends and family thought I had lost a lot of weight but I was not surprised, as the food on that ship just went from bad to worse as the months went by. .

When my leave had expired, I joined a ship called the *Ascania,* an old Cunard liner of 14 000 tons, built in 1925 and now on her last years of service before being broken up. We were on the 'Canadian run' between Southampton, Quebec and Montreal and when stopped in ice fields at night, I would try to imagine what it must have been like for my mother, cramped up in a small lifeboat all night in those freezing conditions. The *Ascania,* being an old ship, had on her bridge as a navigational aid, an old war time radar set which revealed more 'clutter' than anything else and it wasn't too reliable in ice fields. We therefore did, what many ships did in *Titanic's* day and that was to stop when in an ice field, and wait until daybreak, before proceeding up through the Straights of Belle Isle into the Gulf of St Lawrence.

During the early part of the summer, fog and icebergs were always a hazard but regular ice reports had greatly improved over the years for ships on this service. Once these North Atlantic liners had reached an area where icebergs were known to be, ships would operate an ice routine, which meant that all watertight doors would be closed, ports and deadlights shut, lookouts doubled up and the engine room put on standby. Many lessons had been learned from the *Titanic* disaster and this has made the North Atlantic a much safer place as a result.

The *Ascania* being such an old ship, had crew accommodation very much the same as when she was built. The crew's showers and toilets were on the port side and the toilets, about ten of them in all, were in line down one side with only bat wing doors and low side panels for privacy. The waste pipes for these toilets

Cunard Line's ASCANIA.

come out at waterline level and have a 'clacker' at the end, which is a one way valve, and prevents the sea being forced up inside of the pipe in heavy weather.

Being an old ship, many of these 'clackers' had either dropped off or just didn't do what they were supposed to do anymore, making sitting on the ' loo' a hazardous operation. The mornings were the busy time and when the ship pitched into a heavy sea, all the occupants behind those bat wing doors, would raise themselves up off of their seats, one after the other in anticipation of the back draft, followed by a gush of sea water up around their ' rear ends.' Standing at one end of the washroom you could observe all the heads of the occupants coming up and then going down again, one at a time in Mexican Wave fashion. This was usually followed by a bit of cursing and the odd comment about the luxury of getting one's backside washed as part of the daily ablutions.

Apart from some of the drawbacks of crossing the Atlantic in some of the older ships, these voyages across the North Atlantic were popular with seaman. It meant being away from home for only three weeks at a time, making it ideal for those married. My other voyages across the North Atlantic were on the *Queen Mary* and *Queen Elizabeth*, serving on both of those great liners as a paid Lookout man, going over the same course and doing the same job as those that had spotted the iceberg on the *Titanic* back in 1912.

These great liners were not only nearly twice the size of the ill fated *Titanic*, but were much faster, doing the crossing from Southampton to New York in just under five days at a cruising speed of 28 knots. Working on these ships meant we were in closer contact with home life and after a considerable time of serving on these liners, seamen usually ended up working ashore when deciding to call it, 'a day'.

As the decade was coming to an end, my parents had been married for over 40 years by this time and were enjoying a much quieter life without any children at home. My four eldest brothers were away in the Royal Navy, and the fifth married and working for a motor company, the next two younger brothers, were serving in the R.A.F. and I now had two married sisters. Perhaps, one of the advantages of being in a large family such as ours was when most of us were at home on leave together. We would have much to talk about and usually, take our father down the pub in the evenings, although my mother wasn't very keen on the British pub life. Her favourite pastime would be tucking into a box of chocolates or sitting through a movie and that's all she really wanted in life, asking for nothing more. We had our first television set in the late fifties and mother loved it when the odd movie was shown and my father, never one to have any interest in the movies, thoroughly enjoyed the topical news and sports programs.

I would imagine that my parents around this period in their lives were as happy as they had ever been throughout their married life and things were certainly looking up for them. Quite a bit of new furniture had been bought, and my father enjoyed doing a bit of decorating about the place and pottering around in his workshop at the side of the building. The house was cold in the winter and central heating, as we know it today, was not really an option in those days as no one in council accommodation had such luxuries. Apart from the front room, which had a fireplace, there was no heating in the bedrooms and going to bed at night and slipping between icy cold sheets was an ordeal. I can remember on several bitterly cold mornings of picking up my glass of water on the windowsill, inside of the bedroom, and finding a thin sheet of ice on top of it.

If going to bed on a cold night was an ordeal, then getting up in the mornings was equally as arduous, hopping out of bed and scrambling into your clothes as quickly as possible for fear of 'freezing to death.' We usually had a couple of paraffin heaters placed around the other downstairs rooms in the winter months, but these things always gave off that unmistakeable smell of burning paraffin which also dried up the atmosphere. We would place a dish of water on these appliances to overcome the dry atmosphere problem, and also put a perfumed additive in with the paraffin to eliminate some of the smell. Despite all of that, you still knew those things were in use when you walked into someone's home as they still retained their distinctive presence.

Water was heated from behind the fireplace in the front room and a back plate from that was in the dining room, which in turn was supposed to take the chill off of that room but was never very successful in really cold weather. We had a small compact garden at the back with a fishpond, and also a bird aviary in a sheltered corner with several budgerigars and in the summer, it was quite pleasant out there and fairly private. The family pet was a dog called Buster and he had a touch of the Airedale breed about him and although a loveable old thing, he had a nasty habit of chasing motor bikes. We made every effort to keep the dog in as it was dangerous for rider and dog alike but there were times when someone would leave the back door open and on hearing the unmistakable roar of a motor bike, would be out of that house like a shot.

He would tear down the road well ahead of the offending machine and once it caught up with him, he would close in, barking frantically for all his worth as the occasional boot would shoot out from the footrest in an attempt to make a connection with his head. The animal was too smart for that, always being just far enough away to be out of range as he kept pace with the machine.

The dog would return some five minutes later, panting, with his dripping tongue hanging out of the side of his jaw and the look of being absolutely exhausted, but contented nevertheless, having just broken the land speed record for all canines. Of course we would always discipline the animal but he'd had his run, enjoyed a good bark, and made his point about his dislike of motor bikes.

On one such occasion, having almost broken the sound barrier, he collided with our neighbour next door who was just about to crawl under his car with a handful of spanners. On impact, dog, neighbour and spanners went in three different directions, but Buster himself, having rolled over several times, got back on all fours, staggered around a bit and on regaining his bearings, accelerated once again in hot pursuit of the offending motor bike. The neighbour in question, not a happy man at the best of times, attempted to sit up after lying prostrate on the road, and banged his head on the underside of the open car door as he did so. Finally sitting up and rubbing his head, he shouted out in exasperation. ' If I had a gun I'd shoot that bloody dog!' After cooling down a bit, he accepted our apologies, although it took us quite a bit of effort to keep a straight face.

There were times between voyages, when it was 'quiet' living at home as many of my brothers and friends were away and there would be just me and my elderly parents, and not much else going on. I would sometimes go with my father to the British Legion Club where he was on the committee and he managed successfully at one stage, to negotiate my becoming a member. This had been knocked back when an application was made previously, as the ' Legion' only recognised the three armed forces at that time. His argument was that the Merchant Navy had lost more men at sea than the Royal Navy during the war and had been involved in many sea battles in convoys, in their efforts of trying to maintain vital supply routes. He won my case and I became a member, but although grateful for his representations, this kind of club was for the older types that wanted to talk about their experiences in the war with people of their own kind. It wasn't really for us younger people and I couldn't recommend a club like that to anyone that may be hoping to meet with the opposite sex.

Sailing across the Atlantic on the big Cunard liners meant we were in a good position to be able to buy good fashionable 'gear' when in New York.

Clothes for men in those days included the Ivy League suits which were Italian in style, with narrow lapels, short jacket and almost drainpipe trousers, no turn up's and ' winkle picker ' shoes. Other styles we liked were the fingertip full drape jackets, again with trousers that had no turn up's and a good pair of all leather slip on shoes.

One of my favourite outfits was a midnight blue gabardine suit, a 'slim jim tie', or sometimes a 'kipper' tie with a naked lady in a tropical setting on it, a star-dust shirt and blue crepe soled shoes to match. Appearing in that rig out I was almost in techni-colour, and if it had been possible to walk around with a few flashing lights, I would have looked like a Christmas tree. But being a ' flash' dresser at that time was all the rage, especially when the ' Teddy Boy' styles came into being during the fifties. With their really long jackets and velvet collars, boot lace tie and tight drainpipe trousers, massive blue suede shoes with crepe soles, and finished off with a D. A haircut, older people wondered what the world was coming to.

Around June of 1960, a new banana boat arrived in Southampton in prepa-ration for it's maiden voyage, which would entail a regular service between Golfito in Costa Rica and Wilmington in Los Angeles on the west coast of America. The attraction about this voyage was the extra pay of a fixed bonus scheme payable to all crews of British ships on the American coast. This was an opportunity to put some money in the bank, so I decided to find out more about this job and go down to the Shipping Federation Office and see when they were likely to start signing on the crew. Steering well clear of ' Shanghai Jack's office, I managed to get some information from some of the seamen down there who I had sailed with before, this always being the best bet before signing on any vessel, as I had learned from previous experience. The ship was considered a 'good job' according to reports from the 'grape vine' around the docks, and they would only sign on those that had a 'clean' discharge book. A new ship, and a crew with a good disciplinary record seemed to be an attractive proposition, so I decided to give it a go and picked up my documentation, prior to signing on.

It's not always good policy to join a new ship as they can turn out to be 'work houses.' This was mainly brought about by the ship owners wanting as much paint ' slapped ' about as possible on all exposed surfaces to protect the vessel in the early years of its life against the elements. It may well have changed these days with some of these modern protective coverings for exposed metal work, but plenty of paint with a good lead base was the order of the day. at that time.

The *Tenadores* not only had air conditioning and washing machines, but stereo units and a television set in the crews recreation room which up until this time, I had never come across on a ship before. We would be away for 7 months on charter to the United Fruit Company in America but at least we would be reasonably paid and comfortable with it, so I was looking forward to this little ' jaunt. '

After sailing for the West Indies, we picked up a cargo of bananas in Jamaica and took a part cargo to New York before going on to Mobile in Alabama to discharge the rest. We then went back to Kingston in Jamaica and picked up a full cargo for Los Angeles, passing through the Panama Canal. From here on in we would run bananas from Costa Rica to Los Angeles for the next six months. We began to get to know some of the Longshoremen in Wilmington, our discharging port, during these regular voyages and at times, they would invite us home to meet their wives and kids. They were always generous and always showed a lot of interest about life in England after the war, and of course whatever gossip that may have existed, within royal circles. We knew about as much as them on that one, but they always thought that living in that country, we would be able to tell them something they hadn't read about.

Discharging our cargo of bananas in Wilmington one morning we were preparing to paint the funnel. My job was to go up a ladder inside of the funnel

Banana boat TS Tenadores

and once at the top, rig the hooks all the way around the top in order for the bosun's chairs to be used. To enable a person to move up there, a rail is situated all the way around inside, about four feet, or just over a metre from the top, to enable you to move along sideways, clutching the top of the funnel as you go. It was hot up there with several huge exhaust outlets and several steam pipes, some of which are 12 inches in diameter or more.

On your way round you have to pass between some of these steam pipes to make progress around the funnel. I only had a pair of shorts on that morning and after just passing between two steam pipes, there was an almighty explosive roar as super heated steam gushed out of one of the pipes, spewing out boiling water everywhere. I managed to scramble away to the other side, just in the nick of time losing my footing several times as I did so, and coming close to falling down one of the exhaust outlets. Drops of boiling water were raining down all over the place feeling like hot needles as they fell on my bare skin, but that morning my luck was in. Just seconds earlier, I would have had the skin torn from my back when passing between the funnel casing and the steam pipes. The thought of falling down one of those huge exhaust outlets would have been a lousy way to go and you wouldn't wish that on your worst enemy. The bosun, ordered me down right away and gave the First Mate one of the worst ' bollockings' he had probably ever had in his life from a crew member.

As Chief Officer, it was his duty to notify the engine room that men were working on the funnel, but he hadn't done so and it could have cost me my life, him his job and a lot more, if anything had happened to me that morning. In compensation, along with lots of apologies, I was given a bottle of rum, which went down well after we finished the job. The Chief Officer couldn't do enough for me after that, realising how close I had come to losing my life and for a while, even called me by my first name!

Although at first the crew had good credentials when signing on, we all ended up getting 'logged' several times, each time we returned back to the ship late, or missed a watch, losing quite a bit of our wages in fines. This began to add up over the months and some blokes reckoned if it carried on for too long we could end up owing the company money instead of picking up our wages at the end of the voyage.

One night in a bar in Armuelles, this being our loading port, most of us ended up in jail after a bar room brawl which was quite comical. It developed from nothing and in the end we were all having a 'go' as the police arrived, pulling out their guns and truncheons before rounding us all up and shoving us in the back of their ' Paddy Wagon.' On arrival at the jail, we were first of all, relieved of all of our money and cigarettes, which we never saw again, and then thrown into what could only be described as a dungeon. A door was shut behind us which resembled those big heavy doors found on big walk in refrigerators and once shut, you couldn't see your hand in front of your face, being that pitch black inside.

There were no windows so we reckoned it must be some 'hell- hole' used for solitary confinement. It stunk of urine and during the night, just for good measure, several police came in wielding rubber hoses and truncheons just to make sure we all got a good night's sleep. In the morning we didn't look a pretty sight when the First Mate came to bail us out himself, trying to keep a straight face, as he paid a $50 fine for each of us. We were covered in bruises on our arms and legs and sporting a few black eyes between us, apart from stinking to high heaven. Once back onboard, we couldn't wait to get into the showers and delouse ourselves, as some of us by that time, were just about 'crawling' with lice. The Skipper told us later, that the 50 dollars would be coming out of our wages of course, and he also thought, knowing this region, that the local police must have been in a good mood to let us off so lightly.

At the end of our 7 months contract with United Fruit, we headed back through the Panama Canal and went on to Jamaica, again to pick up a cargo, of bananas   for home. There was an urgency to get us loaded as we were approaching Christmas, and we stood a good chance of making it if all went well. We were delayed when we dropped anchor in Bowden, a banana loading port on the Jamaican coast, causing our hopes to be dashed and Christmas looking as far away as ever. In the morning there was a dispute with the loading gangs who were vital in getting the fruit out to the ship in barges, and this took the best part of the day to sort out. Again it was beginning to look hopeless, as nothing was going our way at this stage. Meanwhile, the ship that had priority over us had still not arrived and it was hoped that we could load a cargo before she appeared on the scene.

As luck would have it, the priority vessel was further delayed with engine trouble and our loading commenced and half way through the process, the other ship arrived and dropped anchor in the harbour.

Once the loading was completed, we weighed anchor and got under way, the engineers down below, giving her all she had as it was still touch and go whether we would arrive in time for Christmas. Pounding into heavy seas once past the Azores it was still touch and go whether we could make it for Christmas Eve however, the *Tenadores* did us all proud, steaming along at her maximum speed of 20 knots when the weather permitted, arriving finally in Southampton late Christmas Eve and paying us all off on the morning of December 25.

On picking up our wage accounts and cheques, we noticed that the captain had rescinded all our fines, which was unheard of in our sea going careers up to this point in time, so we all went up to his cabin to thank him and to shake him by the hand. Sitting there with his wife and daughter, he just laughed and said, ' you worked hard and you weren't bad lads, but I had to do something to slow you down a bit!. Just look at it as a Christmas present and have a good leave.' The man was a gentleman and we all reckoned we could sail with him again any time. It was sheer bliss arriving home on Christmas morning after being away for seven months, and we couldn't wait to get home and join in the festivities.

During the fifties, a book had been published titled, ' A Night To Remember', by Walter Lord, and was written in a narrative style about the *Titanic* disaster. Towards the end of that decade, film producer William MacQuitty, decided to work with Walter Lord in the making of the *Titanic* film, ' A night to Remember.' The premier to this film was held at the Odeon Theatre, Leicester Square in London.

On 17 July 1962, the first showing of this film was being held at the Odeon Cinema in Southampton, which was perhaps the best venue for this movie. It was this cinema that was opened back in 1937 by Captain Rostron of the *Carpathia*, the rescue ship to the *Titanic*. My mother, along with some other survivors, namely Fred Fleet, Bert Dean, Eva Hart and Melvina Dean were invited to attend the opening. After seeing the film, the general feeling of those survivors was how closely it resembled the actual tragedy and my mother, in her opinion, had always maintained, it was the most accurate account of that fateful night back in 1912.

In 1996, William MacQuitty presented a signed copy of his book, ' A Life To Remember ' to my mother for her 100th birthday.

In 1961, I had reached the age of 23 and my sea going career was in full swing serving on several ships as a top rate Able Seaman and Quartermaster. Sailing to the West Indies on Elders and Fyffe's banana boats, we would have the problem of stowaways on many of our voyages. They knew the ' ropes ' as it were, realising that the companies outward and homeward bound ships never passed each other on their voyages, always steaming further west on the homeward bound voyage to take full advantage of the gulf stream, thus preventing any transferring of unwanted 'passengers' out at sea. Some twenty four hours after leaving Jamaica, the stowaways would come out of the hatches and give themselves up and we would then have to carry out a strip search in order to find passports if any, and also any offensive weapons they may have on their person. After a shower and a meal we would accommodate them in the forepeak storeroom and put them to work with the rest of us until we arrived in the U.K. These men had nothing and most of them had never had a job in their lives and you had to feel sorry for them.

On arrival in England they would be taken off to jail and wait for the next ship going back out to the West Indies. On release from jail, it was government policy that no prisoner leave prison destitute, so they were kitted out in a complete suit of clothes and given 10 pounds pocket money, which no doubt was a fair bit of money to those men. We would very often take the same stowaways back on the return voyage and they would talk as though they had been on holiday, vowing that they would ' have another go ' the following year.

With a change of direction, in 1961 I managed to get a job that would take me on a seven week South Atlantic cruise, signing on the Royal Mail cruise ship *Andes,* which would be visiting such ports as Lisbon, Montevideo, Rio De Janeiro, Cape Town, Durban and the Canary Islands, on the return voyage. After visiting many of those ports on the outward bound voyage, we called in on a small remote island by the name of Tristan Da Cunha in the South Atlantic, at a position 37% 6' S and 12% 20' W, which had a population of around 250 British, mainly of Scottish descent. It may not be the case today, but at that time, ships on a course that would take them close to this island, would usually be asked to carry mail and a few other items to be unloaded there. The locals would then launch a long boat from the beach and row out to the vessel lying at anchor, weather permitting. The harbour of Tristan Da Cunha is very exposed, and it was always a gamble for the locals to be able to get a boat launched from the beach with a heavy swell running. This happened to be the case when we called in there and after four hours, we had to weigh anchor and continue, leaving the mail in Cape Town on arrival there, until another ship going in that direction, would pick it up and try again.

I mention this island because just a couple of years later, Tristan Da Cunha , was rocked by a powerful volcano and the British government decided that the whole population should be taken off, returned to England and housed at a place called Calshot, just outside of Southampton.

Many of these islanders had never seen a car or television before, and apart from being fascinated by it all, began to enjoy being around these luxury items. Although persuaded to stay in Britain, there being every likelihood that the volcano could erupt again, many of the older people wanted to pick up where they had left off, eventually, going back to their peaceful life, whilst the younger one's elected to remain in Britain.

When we arrived in Cape Town, I went ashore and visited the Mountain View Hotel which my grandfather had owned, and later sold for the princely sum of 14 000 pounds back in 1912, before he, my grandmother and mother, sailed to England to join the *Titanic*. It was a fine hotel in it's day and still looked it, although a bit of a face lift wouldn't have gone amiss I thought, as my gaze wondered around the bar. When speaking to the barman in an effort to glean some information from him regarding the hotel's history since 1912, my enquiries were fruitless. He knew little of its history he said, and the manager who may be able to help was away, which I found quite disappointing after looking forward to this visit for quite some time.

That evening a few of us went ashore to a nightclub and when coming out late at night, we were set upon by a group of 'Skollies' (thugs) with robbery in mind. After a bit of a tussle, and almost having our clothes ripped from our backs, they finally took off realising that we weren't going to be an easy target. It later turned out that I had been stabbed in the affray, but wearing a good tweed jacket at the time probably gave me enough protection from that particular incident. It was the thickness of the jacket and the way that it had gathered up at one stage during the attack, had saved me from more serious injuries.

At the time, my back felt as though there were scratches on it, but closer examination revealed two slits through my jacket and shirt with two corresponding neat cuts just penetrating the skin. On arriving back onboard that night with our clothing dishevelled and torn, we realised that things could have been much worse if we weren't able to take care of ourselves, so thankfully, none of us were the worse for it. One of the other's with us, also had a cut on his forearm, luckily not too much to worry about either, but it was quite clear that our assailants had used a knife and meant business. Thinking back on some of these incidents and other life threatening experiences, you begin to realise just how much of a lottery life really is.

I have always considered it quite remarkable that whilst at sea on passenger ships, we have never had a child fall overboard although many adults have gone over the side, mainly due to attempted suicides. On a voyage to South Africa on the *Athlone Castle*, a young woman was spotted jumping over the rail by one of the crew one morning during wash down. We were in the Bay of Biscay and the weather was fine with just a gentle swell, which was unusual for that time of the year. When the 'man overboard' signal is given, it's usual for the ship to turn 180 degrees to retrace her course and have the engines put on dead slow.

Lookouts are posted up in the bows, up the mast and on the bridge, with everyone scanning the ocean with binoculars. With the sun glinting on the water and all eyes straining to look for someone's head, which is no bigger than the size of a football, it becomes extremely difficult to spot someone in such a vast expanse of water.

Luckily for this young woman, she was spotted right ahead and after stopping, a boat was lowered to pick her up. She was wearing just a dressing gown when they got to her and as they tried to pull her into the boat, amidst her struggles, this slipped off leaving the poor woman stark naked. The struggle was due

Union Castle Line's ATHLONE CASTLE.

to her reluctance to be rescued, but the boat's crew weren't having any of that, and finally yanked her in, minus her dressing gown. She was quickly covered up with a crewmembers shirt before the accident boat came back alongside with several hundred passengers and crew looking on from the upper decks. Attempted suicide victims are usually closely watched throughout the remainder of the voyage and kept in the sick bay until arrival in port.

Whilst we were in Cape Town on this voyage, an elderly foreign seaman who was close to being an alcoholic, went ashore to 'sink' his normal quota of brandy, and on returning to the ship, collapsed on someone else's bunk to sleep it off. Lying on his side, as naked as the day he was born, he exposed his bare backside over the side of the berth. It was clear that at some time during his drinking session ashore, he had visited a lavatory somewhere and being in a bit of a state, had brought back a souvenir. Wedged between the cheeks of his buttocks and sticking out for all to see, was a length of toilet tissue hanging out like a paper tail.

As several of us stood around, having a bit of a laugh over this, there were the odd comments like, ' anyone want to sign their autograph?' and then again, ' any volunteers to pull it out?' The rightful occupant walked around the cabin infuriated. Pointing in the direction of the spectacle lying on his bunk, and stabbing his index finger to emphasise each point, he exclaimed in a strong Welsh accent. ' Disgusting old bastard! ' and then again, ' he wants bloody locking up!'

Standing by the side of his bunk with the seaman snoring like thunder, he was wondering whether to drag him out and shake the hell out of him or leave him to sleep it off. Suddenly, his face lit up as an idea flashed through his mind. Reaching into his pocket, with a look of satisfaction spreading across his face, he proclaimed. 'I'll fix him once and for all!' With that, he pulled his petrol lighter out of his jeans pocket and lit the 'touch paper.' hanging from the prostrate man's backside. We were about to witness our first human torch.

Within a few seconds, as the flames began to lick around the cheeks of his backside, the drunken seaman jumped out of the bunk like he had just been shot from a cannon, dancing about the cabin and waving his hands around his rear end in an effort to cool off his buttocks. He tore out of the cabin without a stitch on, leaving paper ash floating about in his wake, shouting back in broken English. ' Call you'self a 'bladdy' shipmate man!' He then followed it up with just about all the foul language imaginable. It was a bit of a laugh, and when he was sober the next morning, the bloke who's bunk he'd used, told him that the next time he uses a toilet on one of his drunken binges, he should take a pair of scissors with him to prevent any further 'light up's

On one of my voyages to South Africa, I came across a strange coincidence when taking up a conversation with an Irish seaman in a bar in Cape Town. During our chat over a couple of beers, he brought the conversation round to the *Titanic* and his family involvement with that disaster. He went on to say that his grandfather, a young man in his early twenties at the time, was travelling in the third class on that ship and had started a relationship with a young girl who was on her way to New York with her father. After the ship had struck an iceberg, he went on to say that his grandfather had managed to get his new found love into a lifeboat and he himself, ending up in the freezing water clinging to a wooden grating. He was rescued soon after by lifeboat No. 14 and was lucky to get away with his life although he suffered hypothermia and a touch of frost bite.

My mother had always remembered that her boat, being lifeboat No. 14, had picked up four people from the water that night although one of them had later died. One of the other men, according to her mother, sounded like an Irishman muttering incoherently as they wrapped a blanket around his soaked wet shivering body. It was, as we both agreed, quite a coincidence that the two of us sitting in a bar in Cape Town were there that day chatting to each other because the *Titanic* had struck an iceberg.

At the time of hearing this story, I had no idea that one day this whole *Titanic* saga would become so popular as it has today and had never dreamt that one day I would write a book about it. On writing the story about my mother's experiences on that ship, I thought back about that particular conversation in Cape Town and found that it was out of the question to find that Irishman again after 40 years. Of all those 16 lifeboats, including the collapsible boats onboard the *Titanic*, he chose lifeboat No. 14 for his story and having never met me before or knew about my mother's connection with that ship, I never doubted its authenticity. I therefore decided to use this story in my book as a temporary diversion away from the main thrust of my mother's story and gave these two 'love birds' appropriate Irish names.

I had sailed on six different Union Castle Liners to the Cape and each time I had stepped onboard, memories would come flooding back to 1948, and of my excitement at sailing on the *Pretoria Castle* as a ten year old passenger. My infatuation with a young girl by the name of Janice would cause me to smile a bit and also the way my imagination ran riot at that age. My memories of that particular time would be triggered off by that unmistakeable smell all these ships had, of their fruit cargo's wafting about the decks at certain times.

Now having served on these vessels as a crew member, the sheer magic of it had gone forever, although I still had those little ' flashbacks ' to 1948, of a boy's world full of expectations. Those memories would stay with me for many years after but unfortunately, my last voyage to South Africa had finally come to an end as this company, like many other shipping companies, would soon go through great changes.

During the early part of the sixties there were signs that the days of the big liners on regular crossings on the North Atlantic were also coming to an end with the public making greater use of the ever increasing air travel on offer. In the summer months throughout the last decade the big Cunarders would carry anything from between 2 000 and 3 000 passengers on the five day crossing between Southampton and New York. This was now in steady decline and with the running costs of these huge liners continuing to soar, it would only be just a matter of time before this service would run down.

On passages across the North Atlantic on the big White Star liners, 24 hour lookouts were not only posted in the crow's nest but also on the docking bridge aft, this duty known by seamen as the suicide watch. The *Queen Mary* and *Queen Elizabeth* at 81 000, and 83 000 tons respectively, and with their large passenger carrying capacity, had been known on the odd occasion to lose someone over the side. Therefore the docking bridge aft, normally used as a platform for docking purposes, was also an excellent vantage point, being able to view all the decks aft up to the funnel deck.

We were now witnessing the end of this once regular trade across 'the pond' as we knew it, and I, like many others were beginning to realise that jobs in the Merchant Navy would soon be hard to find. These ships alone had a crew compliment of almost 1 500 each so there were going to be a lot of men in the port of Southampton eventually looking for work. This was also going to have it's effect on all support staff ashore and of course the City of Southampton itself. The time was coming for many of us to set our sights in a different direction, and to look for something a bit closer to home. My last voyage to New York was in 1962 on the *Queen Elizabeth* as a paid Lookout Man again, where I would receive an extra two pounds a month and an eyesight test for my efforts. This ship would soon be ending her career and would be taken over by a Chinese magnate by the name of C. Y. Tung who had ideas of turning the ship into a floating university. Unfortunately, it wasn't to be, and after catching fire in Hong Kong harbour, this great liner finally sank and ended up on the sea bed as a total write off. This was no way for a lady to go, although her big sister did better on her retirement, becoming a tourist attraction and convention centre at Longbeach, California.

The last ten years had been quite an interesting period in my life including many voyages into the Mediterranean on cruise ships and serving on troop ships during the Suez Canal crisis. It was time to find work ashore as I was now into a serious relationship and the sound of wedding bells weren't too far away on the horizon.

I tried my hand at various outdoor jobs as I felt that this would help me to settle rather than being in an enclosed environment, I decided to take on a job as a milkman and after one weeks tuition of book work and learning the rounds, I was on my own driving an electric milk cart. Handling this milk float was a 'piece of cake', with a steering wheel and just two pedals to operate, that of an accelerator and the other as a brake. There were some tight little cul –de- sacs to negotiate and with a minimum of skill, one could turn the vehicle completely around in a tight circle in one operation if you judged it right. After my training, I was ready to go solo and couldn't wait to hit the road feeling as free as a bird and also being in charge of my day's work, which is all I wanted.

After a few days, my confidence was building and on arrival at a tight cul -de –sac with particularly high kerbing on each side, I swung the vehicle around in an attempt to do the turn in one continuous movement without stopping. As I swept around in an arc, and quickly came up on the opposite side of the road, a sickening feeling came over me as I could see that I just wasn't going to make it. Completely out of control by this time, and not experienced enough to take quick evasive action, I struck the kerb with a hard glancing blow. This was instantly followed by hundreds of bottles of milk, still in their crates being jetti-soned across the road with the sound of smashing bottles and milk splashing all over the place.

With broken glass everywhere and milk pouring down the drains, doors and windows began to open to see what had caused such a disturbance in this nor-mally quiet neighbourhood. I immediately took stock of the situation and decided perhaps there wasn't a future for me as a milkman after all. After a phone call to the dairy, they sent out a truck with some blokes to help to clear up the mess and on their arrival, I handed over my cash and books before they could utter a word, and told them to keep it.

Other jobs I tried were gas meter reader, postman, and baker's rounds man, but as always   none of those jobs were anything like you imagined them to be, apart from hard work, poor pay and predominantly bad weather conditions. I needed to get into a job that paid well and do something that I was trained for which meant, I would finally end up once more being a seaman. I applied for a job as an Able Seaman with the Red Funnel Company working on their ferries, and was taken on again, where it had all started for me as a Deck Boy some ten years previously. This gave me the stability I needed when I married Leann, my first wife in March 1963, and I would settle down in this job for the next three years, and we would start a family.

> *I can never forget my first trip to sea,*
> *and the things I was expected to do.*
> *There were decks to scrub and meals to get*
> *and thrusting my arm down a loo.*
>
> *There were ropes to splice and knots to tie*
> *and whippings to go on rope ends.*
> *But when it came to unblocking the loo,*
> *my arms wouldn't go round the bends.*
>
> Haisey.

Chapter Four
A Tragic Beginning

After we became married, my new wife and I moved in with my parents for a short while until mortgage requirements had been finalised. We then moved into a maisonette in Thornhill, an eastern suburb of Southampton. To qualify for mortgages in those days, one had to be in a job for a considerable time and the employer would have to endorse the fact that you had a steady job and a future with the company. Other criteria required, would be that your weekly wage would not be less than the monthly payment due, which was designed to prevent the borrower from taking on more than they could afford.

The property we bought was new, on the ground floor, and being on a corner plot, had a fair sized garden. Before being allowed to move in, we had to wait for a considerable time until the builders were satisfied that the property had dried out sufficiently before habitation. We were growing impatient as my wife was now pregnant with our first child and we really wanted the birth to be in our new home. In those days home births, assisted by a midwife, were a choice by mothers and quite common at that time, as long the pregnancy appeared to be normal. The home where the birth was to take place was also taken into consideration, as long as reasonable conditions existed for the child to be born there.

When finally moving into your first home, there's a great feeling as ideas abound as to what goes where and what doesn't go where and so on, and its all enjoyable stuff because you can do what you like. Unfortunately, I worked such long hours in those days that when I finally had a day off, there was much to catch up on and putting ideas into practice very often never materialised. Travelling to work in those days was by bicycle and hard going at times, especially during the winter months with black ice on the roads. I can remember on the occasion when cycling to work, one of the wheels would slip and the bike would slide one way, and I would end up flat on my back sliding in another direction.

The cycling to work would take about 30 minutes on average, and much longer, coming home with the journey being up hill all the way. After a 16 hour day, cycling up those hills on the way home wasn't much to look forward to and at times, I wondered if it was all worth it. The money was good, but working on the ferries still meant long hours, which still hadn't changed from the time when I was a Deck Boy with the company, back in the fifties. I would leave home at 5 am and return the following night at 9pm throughout most of the year and although this job gave me the chance to own our home, I had little time to spend in it.

After being in our maisonette for a short time, it soon became clear that the place was still damp and being wintertime, it didn't help matters much. We tried to dry the place out with the use of fan heaters but the walls seemed to sweat all the more, so it soon became clear that my wife would have to have the baby at her mother's house. We were totally to blame for this due to our impatience and wanting to move in against the builder's advice.

During this first year of our marriage there had been some extraordinary events that had taken place. In August the newspapers were full of The Great Train Robbery and in October, everyone appeared to be in the grip of ' Beatlemania ' In November the whole world was stunned after hearing of the assassination of President Kennedy in Dallas. It is said that everyone knows where they were when hearing that news and in my particular case that's true, as I remember being alongside an oil jetty during refuelling of our ship the *Vecta*. We all thought at that time that there may well have been a Russian plot due to the Cuban crisis and as a result, all hell was going to break loose, but luckily that never happened.

On the 26 February1964, my wife gave birth to a beautiful son and we named him David, after me his father, and his second name William, after my wife's father. The feelings I had when I saw our boy for the first time were those of absolute wonder and happiness, something that I had never experienced before. Those special feelings were to come back again at the birth's of our other children so perhaps, Mother Nature, has a secret formula for such occasions. We were so proud that day and our boy was going to have a far better life than we ever had, and we would do many things together.

Whilst working on the ferries, we endured one of the worst winters we have ever known in England with pack ice floating around the docks and a freeze up that lasted for three months, starting with a blizzard on Boxing Day 1964. A bitterly cold easterly wind blew for most of that time and icicles were seen to be hanging off of the jetties and wharves around the docks, never thawing throughout that period. I can always remember my feet always being cold and wearing several pairs of socks in the process. I wore two pairs of trousers and a woollen pullover instead of a vest as most seamen would agree, wearing wool against the skin if you can stand it, is the best way to keep in the warmth. The backs of my hands were chapped and raw, feeling like sandpaper due to the job I did onboard which was working the ' back spring ' in the bow, usually with frozen ropes and lines.

When those ferries came alongside the berth, they would have a fair bit of 'way' on them and the seaman in the bow, would use quite a bit of skill, along with good ' heaving line ' accuracy and rope work, to assist in pulling the vessel up. Gloves would be hazardous in a situation like this as most seaman like to 'feel' the rope they're working with, and working with ice in the rope a great deal of the time, the end result was bloody sore hands.

I was becoming restless although we now had our own home and had started a family, life just seemed to be all work with little pleasure and I was seriously thinking of working ashore. I began to envy people that could get up in the mornings at a civilized hour, work for eight or nine hours each day for five days a week and have weekends at home with their families.

My third eldest brother Geoff, had been finding it difficult to settle after leaving the Royal Navy, although he had sailed with me on voyages to Canada in the hope that the Merchant Navy may give him a better life. He always said however, and I wholeheartedly agreed with him, that a seaman's life is no good if you are married. After all, it's why you marry in the first place, that of being together. He wasn't happy being away and couldn't settle in a job at home so he decided to ' take the bull by the horns' and apply to migrate to Australia. My eldest sister Joy, who had just recently divorced, and had also been 'bitten by the bug ', decided that perhaps, Australia would offer her and her young children a better life so she also applied to emigrate, and later arrived a short while after her brother, in Brisbane.

My father was a man that always had to have something to occupy his mind and now that he was retired, he was showing signs of becoming restless as well, possibly by the moves the other's had made. He used to love to potter around in the outhouse, but in the winter months it was a 'no go' area being, just too cold to do anything outside for long. He began to see Australia as a country where he could settle down and retire and it goes without saying, there was a feeling that perhaps, this could be a life similar to the one that they had enjoyed so much in South Africa almost 20 years ago. The idea of emigrating was becoming implanted in the minds of many of us and I think the ' wonder lust' we all had must certainly have come from our father. I always thought at that time, as I do now, that my mother would have been happy to have stayed where she was, as she had gone through a great deal of upheaval in her life, having given birth, and then raising ten children, along with being forever on the move.

My parents were probably more settled now after 15 years in this house, than they had ever been throughout their married lives and coupled with that, they now had a nice home. I was never to know the real deciding factor behind their move but once the decision was made, I must admit that I was very surprised to see that they were going through with emigration at their age. However, their minds were made up and they were once again going to sell up everything and emigrate to Australia following the other members of our family already out there. A move like that, takes a considerable amount of courage especially being pensioners, because if things go wrong, then they have little to fall back on. This again had its predictable' knock on' effect with the rest of us beginning to seriously consider Australia as the place to make new lives for ourselves. I had already visited Australia back in the fifties as a young seaman, speaking to several emigrants out there at that time, and their collective opinions were very favourable about living in that country.

When at home between voyages, I had bumped into my shipmate Bob several times and I had also sailed with him on a few ships throughout my seagoing days, but not so with Froggy. He had apparently disappeared off of the face of the earth over these later years and no one seemed to know of his whereabouts. Bob on the other hand, was like one of the family when he was around and would pop in at home whenever he was on leave. He was a bit of a character and comedian without ever knowing it, mainly by his actions and spur of the moment, decision making. His upbringing was that of a broken home, and coming from a huge family, hardly knew any of them as they were all put into care. I can never forget some of the stories he told me about those boy's homes during the war years and the hard times and cruelty that he had endured. I can recall both of us going to our local pub, The Bitterne Brewery, one night and shortly after arrival, started chatting up a couple of girls in the bar. We soon learned that these girls were from St Teresa's, a hostel for homeless young women situated not far from us in the West End Road. As our conversation got to the stage of asking ' who comes from where?' and ' What are you doing here?' We found to our amazement that one of the girls was Bob's younger sister. The look on everyone's faces after that revelation was a real picture and needless to say, the end of the 'chatting up ' process for that particular evening.

On another occasion we were invited to my brother Donald and his wife Anne's house for a meal one day and Bob elected to go out to buy the steaks whilst we had a few drinks waiting for him. We never saw him again until 3 months later after paying off of a ship when finally arriving back home. It appears he fell foul of ' Shanghai Jack ' when dropping in to the Shipping Federation and ended up packing his bags after being ' press ganged ' into joining a ship that very same day. There was always an unwritten law for seamen and that was if you had any immediate plans for your home life, steer well clear of the Shipping Federation.

My living standards by this time had improved slightly and I was now in a position to buy a new Honda 50 motor cycle which in turn, would give me a break from all that cycling going to, and from work. As for Bob, he was also fed up with hopping onto buses and decided to invest in one as well and we found them to be useful little ' runabouts.' Although our bikes were identical, Bob had always insisted that his was faster than mine and like some big kid, thought he would prove his point, overtaking me one evening just before it got dark. He tore down the road behind me and then on overtaking, gave me the ' V ' sign as he approached a sharp bend at the bottom. Going fast enough to give Concorde a run for its money, he arrived at the bend far sooner than he thought and as a result misjudged it. After skidding sideways, amidst clouds of dust and dirt, shooting gravel all over the place, he finally ended up in someone's front garden, ripping out plants and shrubs as he went. When I caught up with him, he was sitting on the lawn laughing, rubbing his head and looking a bit dazed, his Honda only visible in the flowerbeds by the sight of one of the wheels still slowly turning. With no injury apparent, I almost fell off of my bike with laughter as he spluttered out in urgency , ' I told you my bike was faster! Now come on, let's get out of here!'

With that, I helped him drag his machine out of the flower beds before anyone had seen us and scrambled back onto the road, laughing like a couple of school boys.

With the little leisure time we had together, my wife and I would sometimes go to a bowling club on a Saturday evening with her parents. At other times an evening out in a comfortable pub somewhere with family and friends was also another pastime we all enjoyed when the opportunity presented itself. We had few holidays in those days but when we were lucky enough to be able to afford one, it was usually taken on the Isle of Wight or in the West Country. A new pop group had come on the scene during this year, known as The Rolling Stones and they and the Beatles were to become one of the few ' long -stayers ' in the pop industry. In June of 1964, the Beatles visited Adelaide amid the usual hysteria that seemed to follow the group wherever they went and songs like 'She Loves You' and 'From Me To You ' were forever being played on the airwaves. These groups had taken the world by storm with their particular style of music and were bringing about a change from the domination of the music scene by the Americans.

In December of 1964, my mother and father sailed for Australia on the P&O liner *Oriana,* and arrived in Brisbane on 14 January 1965. Before their departure from Southampton, the Southern Daily Echo, the local newspaper, interviewed my mother and they consequently ran an article in their evening edition, reporting that one of the last *Titanic* survivors was leaving England to settle in Australia.

On arrival at Brisbane, my mother and father were met by the family already living there and also the Courier Mail, Brisbane's main newspaper, who ran an article along with a photo in their paper the next day, regarding the *Titanic* connection.

On 21 February 1966, our second son was born and we named him Andrew with his second name being Fredrick , this being taken from my father. His arrival was quite an experience for me, as the midwife attending said I could be present at the birth if I wished, so I accepted and never forgot it. Andrew was born in our maisonette in Priestwood close so at least one of our children had been born in our first home, which is what we always wanted. Little David now had a brother and we had two lovely sons, causing us to feel ' over the moon ' as they say, with our growing little family

Our applications to emigrate were soon to be processed and it wouldn't be long before we would be on our way to Australia, travelling with my wife's sister and husband who had also decided to give it a go. These two sons of ours were the only grandchildren my in laws had and we fully realised the impact this would have on leaving, but we had to get on with our lives and they fully accepted that.

We finally received a departure date and immediately put our home on the market, as this was the over riding factor of when we would be able to go. The person that was interested in buying our property had known that we were emigrating and tried every tactic to hold things back in an effort to force us into reducing the asking price. We weren't going to make much out of the sale anyway as house prices in those days rose only slightly each year, so we decided to ' hang in there' and give nothing away. This sharp practice by their solicitors made those final weeks of waiting a nightmare, knowing that if we were to withdraw from the sale, it would delay us even further. We finally signed over on the day before sailing, and picked our cheque up at the bank, by special arrangement with our solicitor, after they had closed for business that day.

My mother and father with granddaughter Dawn on arrival in Brisbane
—Courtesy COURIER MAIL

Finally our departure date was set and we would be sailing on Sitmar Line's, *Fairsky* from Southampton's Western Docks. The other vessel on the emigrant service with this company was the *Fairsea* and both ships were fully booked on every voyage as we were now approaching the mid sixties, with emigration to Australia in full swing. On sailing day, my wife's father and her uncle who both worked in the docks, made arrangements with people they knew, to ensure our boarding the vessel went smoothly with the minimum of waiting time. This gave us an advantage over other people embarking, and with young children, it was a great help.

On sailing that day, it was a sad occasion for my wife and her sister and of course their parents, never knowing when they would ever see each other again. They weren't alone, as thousands of emigrants must have been going through this same heartache, week in and week out, and it's just one of the many sacrifices you have to go through in search of hopefully, a better life for yourselves and children.

We sailed around midday as I recall, and my first impression of the ship was that it was smaller than at first thought and very much overcrowded. Having previously sailed on many passenger ships including emigrant ships, I would go so far as to say that, comparing this ship with those others, this vessel had far too many people onboard. Apart from the overcrowding, the Italian crew did their best, the meals were quite good and so was the entertainment, although we had to get into the main lounge early in the evenings in order to get a seat   We met many friends onboard including one of them who was a nurse by the name of Janine and it was this name, that inspired us to call our daughter Janina, when she finally entered the world a couple of years later.

During the voyage, children's evening meals were served an hour before adults and their parents would take them down to the dining saloon at around 5pm. This went well for us at the beginning of the voyage but later on, David had great difficulty in keeping his food down, vomiting after every meal. At first we thought he had picked up a stomach bug but it went on for too long and on consultation with the ship's doctor, he mentioned something about some young children not being able to travel well. It wasn't until arrival at Freemantle that David had been able to enjoy a meal without all of us wondering if it was going to come back up again, so perhaps the ship's doctor had been right after all.

This voyage took us past Gibraltar, into the Mediterranean, onto Port Said, through the Suez Canal, and then into the Red Sea. We called in at Aden for a few hours, and went ashore, strolling around a few of the bazaars before boarding again and setting sail into the Indian Ocean, finally arriving at Freemantle some four weeks after leaving Southampton. For those that had never travelled abroad before, it must have been a bit of an experience for them to see so much of the world, although many passengers disappeared below decks for a few days, suffering from sea sickness, once we had entered into the Indian Ocean.

At Fremantle, immigration officers boarded the ship and would stay onboard to interview passengers as we sailed around the Australian coast calling in at Melbourne and finally, Sydney where we disembarked. We boarded a train for the overnight journey to Brisbane and on arriving, were met by several members of our family. We would be staying in Ridge Street, at Highgate Hill in Brisbane until we found other accommodation and also, until I had found a job.

We were here at last, and all our hopes and aspirations with a bit of luck, could now begin to take shape with the many opportunities Australia had to offer. Our plans were naturally for me to find suitable work and then think about a mortgage and begin to build a home and a better life for the four of us. The weather was ideal for the children to spend most of their time outdoors, splashing about in their back yard swimming pools and for those trips to the coast. We all sought to get a tan, worshipped the sun and hadn't heard of such things as sun block, skin cancers or holes in the ozone layer. Coming home after a day down the beach, feeling hot and uncomfortable after too much sun was all part of a good day out and we couldn't wait to get another dose of the same the following week.

I found a couple of quick jobs, the first, as a postman with a bicycle as the only means of transport. When delivering mail, the postman had to blow a whistle to let the resident know that a letter had been delivered. This also let all the dogs in the neighbourhood know that you were around as well, so after being chased a few times, I gave it up as a bad job. The other job was in a glass factory, working on a conveyor belt, stacking bottles into cardboard cartons and was so repetitious, as to the point of being soul destroying, along with the place being an absolute sweat shop as well. Clearly, one day I would have to settle into a shore job but not just yet, so I decided to set my sights on a sure thing until we were a bit more settled. Once again I went in search of finding a ship, and doing what I had been trained for all my working life up to this point in time. My application to join the Harbours and Marine dredge fleet was successful and I started working on the Brisbane River onboard the mud hopper *Cowrie,* supporting the dredger *Groper,* on a rocks cutting across the river.

This turned out to be a good job with civilized hours and weekends off, making me feel reasonably settled and thought that the time may be right to start making plans of buying our own home eventually. Other work on the river involved crewing up on an old suction dredger named the *Echeneis* and some time later, when both of these old dredgers were ready to be scrapped, they were taken out into Morton Bay and sunk just off of Morton Island to form a lagoon type environment at the island. Whilst working with the dredge fleet I bought a 'Holden' car, an Australian make, and took my driving test which was carried out by the police in those days, and after driving around many tram routes in the city, I passed my test.

Our first six months in Australia were taken up with moving into another property in Audenshaw Street at Highgate Hill and getting out and about around Brisbane in general. Both of our sons, David and Andrew were having a good life up to this time and were both certainly a picture of health. Around the end of May 1967, David became what only could be described as ' touchy ', which was so unlike him as he was usually such a happy, good natured, child. He was also becoming pale, losing that good colour he always had and at the time we thought it may well be his becoming run down after all the upheaval of the past year.

On 15 June, we took him to see a doctor, as we were a bit concerned, and to our surprise, told that David was anaemic and a course of iron would be pre-scribed for him to be taken over the next month. We were also told at that time that this wasn't uncommon in young children and the treatment would soon bring back the colour to his cheeks.

I can't say that we were happy with the way things were looking and after a few more days, I decided to see the doctor again about David's condition. I was told that it's normal for parents to worry over a condition like simple anaemia, but I should dismiss any thoughts of his condition being any more serious than it really was. Five days later, the boy developed a serious nosebleed which we could not stop despite our efforts and finally, phoned the doctor who failed to turn up anyway. The nose bleed did stop after a very long time and it was clear that he had lost a lot of blood throughout this ordeal which in turn, caused us a great deal of anxiety. Within the next two weeks he continued to deteriorate after being treated for tonsillitis and a persistent cough, and if that wasn't enough, he now also had great difficulty in walking. The bruising that had appeared on his arms and legs were further indications to us that things were getting quite serious and we needed some quick answers. Another visit from the doctor at the end of the month revealed that in his opinion, David was suffering from pernicious anaemia and would need to go on a course of iron as the prescribed treatment so far, just wasn't having any effect.

On my mother and father's 50th wedding anniversary, we all went to Ridge Street for a celebration but for us, celebrating was the last thing on our minds with everyone saying how poorly David looked. There was plenty of advice like, ' get another opinion ' and ' take him straight to hospital ' or ' get a blood count ' all good advice no doubt and of course everyone meant well, but it didn't make us feel any better. By the first week in July, our patience had run out and we made alternative arrangements to have an immediate blood count taken, with the result being given to our own doctor afterwards. A day or so later, I phoned up for the results of the test and discovered that it was the doctors day off, so we had to wait for another agonising day to find out what was happening to our son.

When finally getting hold of the him the next day, he told me that I had better go down to his surgery as he needed to talk to me and on my arrival there, I was shown straight into his consulting room. He offered me a cigarette and asked me to take a seat before coming straight to the point and saying. ' I'm afraid David has leukaemia'   He went on, ' my diagnosis could be wrong so I'm referring him to a specialist.' I sat in his surgery completely stunned, not believing what I was hearing about our son. There must be a mistake I thought and then, as though reading my mind, he went on to say in his slightly broken English. ' Doctor Felix Arden is the best there is when it comes to the treatment of leukaemia in children and I have already made an appointment for you to see him.'

With that, I left his surgery in a state of shock and now had the grim task of telling my wife what I had just learned about David's condition. On the way home, I was close to tears with a lump in my throat as my thoughts were racing through my mind on how to deal with this. There was the feeling of helplessness and of which way to turn in order to get the best possible treatment for our son. We must get all the information available I thought, take him to America or anywhere else for that matter, but we must do something.

Driving home that day was something I could never remember and if I had gone through a few stop signs on the way, I never realised it, but I do remember seeing my wife standing at the front door as I came into the driveway. When I got to her, I didn't have to say anything, as she knew by the look on my face that the worst had happened. She then burst into tears as we just stood there, holding on to each other, our lives shattered.

Doctor Arden, originally from England, was a known, respected paediatrician, and at his surgery in Wickham Terrace in Brisbane, the diagnosis was confirmed. David was suffering from acute lymphoblastic leukaemia and would need to enter hospital immediately for blood transfusions and the relevant prescribed drugs. This was a week that we would never forget when also told, that in his present condition he had about two weeks to live and with proper care and treatment, the bleak prognosis revealed that his life expectancy was about 18 months.

Great Ormond Street Children's Hospital in London had a good reputation during those days, in the treatment of childhood leukaemia although we were rightly told, that treatment in Australia and many other parts of the world was identical. We decided to return to England, bearing in mind that my two sons were the only grandchildren my wife's parents had, and taking our son to England and perhaps on to London for further treatment, gave us the feeling of 'doing something.' Unfortunately for us, we had not been in Australia for the two year term that was laid down to all emigrants which stipulated, that returning to the U.K. before that period had expired, meant repaying the full outward bound fare.

We sought help from several Senators and of course, Doctor Arden who very kindly wrote a letter of support for us to the Chief Migration Officer in Canberra.

Back in England, the family over there were doing all they could by writing to their local M.P, The Speaker of The House Of Commons and also the Red Cross. Whilst David was in the Brisbane Children's Hospital, we had a visit from the press and where they got the story from was always going to be a mystery to us. They asked us many questions about David and what our plans were, finally taking several photos of him sitting up in bed holding one of his teddy bears. On the following Sunday, in Brisbane's most popular newspaper, ' The Sunday Truth', David was front page news alongside of a beautiful picture of him, and underneath the caption, 'Just a few months to live.' This was heart rending to read this but the publicity helped us to get things moving and within a few weeks we had a letter from the Migration Department granting us a waiver, allowing us to return to the U.K. without paying a penalty.

As a result of the front page coverage of The Sunday Truth, we were never to forget the tremendous support and kindness shown from so many of their readers and those work mates of mine on the Brisbane Dredge Fleet that just couldn't do enough for us at that time.

Among the many letters we received, some were extremely touching like the very old man who enclosed a ten shilling note saying, that he had cut out David's photo from the newspaper and will put it with all the things that he treasures the most. Another from a schoolboy enclosing his pocket money saying that he hopes it will go towards making David a little bit happier. We answered every letter thanking them and have kept most of them to this very day.

After four weeks in hospital, David had come into remission and was looking like his old self again much to our relief although still very shaky on his legs. We were given the ' all clear ' for him to travel so we went ahead and booked our flight with Pan Am, leaving Brisbane on 21 August.

On arrival back in the U.K. David was news in the local press and once again, there were many letters from readers and many of our friends calling on us to see how we all were. After handing in David's case history at the Southampton Children's Hospital, his new specialist carried out a further examination, revealing that the boy was doing extremely well and he wouldn't need to see him for another month.

As always, life must go on so after moving in with my wife's parents I had to go out and find work, finally ending up in a factory, working on a lathe, turning out castings. This was interesting work at times but also repetitive like most factory work but I had little choice, as we needed the money and would have to start a new home again. I remained in this job for almost a year and for the first part of that time, David had appeared so well that some people began to question whether he was suffering from this dreadful disease at all. It got into the newspapers again and one such article was titled. 'Leukaemia clear verdict on boy '

The local authority allocated us a home in Meggeson Avenue at Townhill Park in Southampton, and this was a great relief for us from the continual writing of letters and phone calls, as we could now give the two boys that extra freedom they so much needed. We had a joint party on 26 February for David's fourth and Andrew's second birthdays which were only five days apart. On 24 March 1968, my wife gave birth to a beautiful girl and we named her Janina Carolyn. We were overjoyed at having a girl, and this diverted our attentions away from the two boys for a while as the pair of them were 'little monkeys' at times, now that David was so well.

It wasn't to last however, as shortly after this good spell, he ended up in hospital again and later, on three other occasions, fighting for his life and undergoing massive blood transfusions. Each time on remission he was that much weaker and huge doses of drugs were administered to keep him going.

On Wednesday 25 September, I went into the boy's bedroom as usual and noticed David lying quietly in his bed staring up at the ceiling, giving me a half smile as I kissed him and Andrew before leaving for work. Later that morning I received a phone call to say that my wife was at the hospital with David as he had gone into a coma. We spent the next three days and nights at his bedside, holding his hand and talking to him, but there was little response. On Saturday, 28 September at 1pm, our beautiful son aged just 4 years and seven months had finally lost his battle for life and had quietly passed away.

It was at a time like this that I wished I could have found some solace from religion like my wife and others around us, but I was never that way inclined, however I would like to have thought that the following words may have meant something at that time.

A little child was given. The happiness was brief. The joy he brought into our lives was turned to bitter grief, He was taken, we were left to face the years ahead, with broken hearts and empty arms, but somehow we were led, through the storms of sorrow, to the quiet certainty, that one day we shall see beyond the veil of tragedy, and understand the workings of a plan not yet revealed. Time will work the miracle and every wound will be healed. Still we mourn him sadly, but the days in passing bring, the faith that we shall meet again, in God's eternal spring.

—Patience Strong.

David junior at the Brisbane Children's Hospital shortly before flying back to England.

Chapter Five
Another Start

Whilst back at work one morning, two of my old shipmates walked into the factory and came over to where I was working and one of them said. ' Come on mate, you've been through enough and this is no bloody place for man or beast! We've got a job for you back in the old outfit, so tell them to stuff it and get out of here!'

This meant of course that I would be returning to the Red Funnel Ferry service once again, and the way I was feeling about work and life in general that morning, I couldn't have heard better news! I gave my notice in that morning and left a few days later to join a hydrofoil, one of the latest high speed vessels, now being used by the Red Funnel company on their island service. Apart from the welcome change of employment, the wages were far better, over twice as much as in the factory and once again, we could set our sights on starting to get a home together again.

In the late sixties, the housing authorities were selling homes to tenants, taking into consideration the rent paid during the tenancy, which made some of these properties a real bargain. We put in for our house, like many other tenants at that time, as we were well pleased with the area in general and the house itself. It was a good feeling to have our own place again and felt the time was right to settle down and get back into living a normal life.

On 30 July1969, my wife gave birth to our fourth child, another lovely girl and we named her Janette Suzanne. It was said by several people that Janette was our ' replacement child ' but I think we've always known that we would have had her, whether we had lost David or not. We all knew that she and our other children were a tremendous help, and perhaps vital for my wife and I to get back to some sort of normality in our lives. By just having them around us, and allowing them to take up most of our time, was perhaps all the therapy one needed to get over that tragic period. The end of this decade was upon us and it was a time in our lives that may well be best forgotten but as it's been said many times before, time is a great healer.

During the winter of 1969, my mother and father returned to England after five years in Australia, deciding that they wanted to end their days in the 'Old Country.' They arrived on a bitterly cold day in the middle of a power strike and moved in with my wife and I until other accommodation could be found. My mother and father were now 74 and 76 years of age respectively and would now have to start all over again with only their pension to do it on. They were eventually allocated a warden controlled old peoples flat in Westwood Road in Portswood and by a remarkable coincidence, when standing in a certain position on their balcony, you could see the house in Winn Road where Captain Smith of the *Titanic* used to live.

Working on the hydrofoil ferry service, involved doing the same thing day in and day out, almost as though being on a bus, but after a short time I was back on the car ferries which was a more interesting aspect of the job. At the end of August 1969, the Isle of Wight Pop Festival got under way and our ships carried literally thousands of people and their cars across to the island in order to join in the festivities. Arriving at the docks were motorised caravans and campers, motorcycles, and vehicles of all descriptions from all over the world. Without any doubt, many of these longhaired, bearded ' pop' followers had plenty of money, which was apparent from the transport they were using and the different countries they had travelled from just to attend this event. The collection of vehicles on our car decks each trip was mind boggling and any ' petrol head ' would have had a field day just walking around inspecting the different modes of transportation being used.

When arriving onboard in a vehicle, it was company policy that all passengers should leave their cars for safety reasons. Once the car was parked, we would usually open the doors for the passengers to help them out and on some occasions, the smell of 'wacky- baccy' wafting about the car decks, was enough to knock us off our feet. On getting out of their vehicles, they were usually dressed in either caftans, jeans, army or air force greatcoats, long dresses and shawls on the women, and many of them seen to be wearing colourful bandanna's tied about their heads.

With numerous beads around their necks and some tied in their hair, they would say things like 'peace brother' or 'cool man', following that by holding up two fingers in a victory sign. With some of the men, you were able to detect an eye now and then under their long hair, which cascaded down over their heads and shoulders, becoming almost one continuous ' thatch' as it joined up with their long bedraggled beards. As you directed them from their cars and up to the open decks, you became increasingly aware that these were a peaceful happy bunch of human beings, in search of their particular kind of company and music and everything else that goes with this kind of event.

The many famous stars attending the festival included Bob Dylan, Jane Fonda and Roger Vadim along with many other popular groups turning this into a most sought after worldwide event. On one of our trips to the island, we had a full complement of police with their squad cars and motor cycles to help the island police force in controlling the 150 000 avid pop fans. In August 1970, there was a repeat performance of the Isle of Wight Pop Festival and once again the ferry companies did extremely well out of it.

After the festival was over, we brought them all back again with some of them taking on the appearance of total ' wrecks,' having indulged in all that was on offer but it was quite clear, that a good time was had by all. The following month, Jimi Hendrix was reported to have died from a drug overdose in London. This was also the year that the Beatles had decided to ' call it a day ' as a group, and went their own separate ways.

Serving on these ferries was a lot of fun at times despite the long hours and apart from meeting the many interesting people throughout this period, some of the crew were real characters.

Our cook onboard was a likeable, grossly over weight bloke, with the nick name of 'Oily Ollie ' and was well known to use his hands for just about everything when working in the galley. He was short, had hair like straw and wore pebble glasses, which at times, were about as much use to him as a chocolate teapot, especially when they got steamed up in the galley. He had huge hands, which resembled shovels and would push the food around on your plate with the delicate touch of a mechanical digger, licking his fingers in the process. Once he was satisfied that your meal looked presentable, he would wipe the gravy off the edges of the plate with a heavily stained grey tea towel hanging from his waist. With sweat and oil oozing from every pore he would then hand your food over to you through the galley hatchway as though you were about to receive a touch of cordon bleu.

I can remember the captain at breakfast one morning saying. ' Just one egg for me this morning please Ollie ' as he placed the captain's breakfast on the table in front of him. ' Very well sir,' said Ollie, as he returned   to the stove, and ran a huge horned thumbnail between the two fried eggs that were joined together. With a flick of his thumb, one egg was hurtled almost a metre, back into the frying pan without breaking the yoke. The captain looked horrified at what he had just seen and said to him. ' Don't you ever use a spatula Ollie? ' The cook, with his eyes hardly recognisable from behind his misted up glasses, smiled as he replied. ' Oh no sir. I'm used to it. It doesn't burn at all!' ' Oily Ollie' thought he was right up there with the best of them when carrying out these little culinary skills of his and was extremely proud of some of his methods.

Another experience that was worth witnessing was when Ollie was putting cream over apple pie or something similar. Instead of using a piping bag, he would thrust one of his huge hands into the mixing bowl full of cream and grab a fist full. With all the pudding bowls lined up, he would hold his fist over each dish and do a quick half circular flick with his wrist and like magic, a perfect pinnacle of cream would appear on each plate as he moved his hand along the line. After this little trick, he would usually wipe his hands on that dirty old tea towel around his waste and afterwards you could see blobs and smears of cream all over the pots and pans. Surprisingly, his meals were very tasty and well cooked, but if you didn't want to spoil your appetite before meals, it was advisable not to watch him at work in the galley. He was a most obliging bloke and sometimes when you were eating your meal, he would walk into the mess room and 'plonk ' an extra roast potato on your plate, with his hands of course.

Working on Southampton Water in those days was an interesting period being such a busy port with no two days ever the same with ships of all nationalities arriving and leaving on a daily basis. The *Q. E. 2*, which was launched by the queen in September of 1967, was now a regular caller in the port of Southampton between cruises, and was replacing the *Queen Mary*, which had finally completed her last transatlantic voyage.

The arrival and sailing of these great liners in the port were always a tourist attraction during the summer months as there were many good vantage points around the docks and on the piers. The best way to see these ships would be from the decks of the ferries, when operating between Cowes on the Isle of Wight, and Southampton. There were many interesting landmarks on this route, including historic buildings, castles and pretty countryside, which encouraged many of the general public to do a round trip to take in the scenery.

Apart from the great liners, there was an abundance of small craft using the waterways including the sand and gravel ships and sludge tankers. These sludge tankers would take raw sewage out of the port and dump it outside of the three mile limit on a daily basis and at times, when on the lee side of them, you would get a good 'whiff' of their cargo as they passed you on the river.

Black bearded Jerry, one of our crew, had a good sense of humour especially when talking to passengers and always managed to keep a straight face. Being a bit of an old sea dog, many people believed what he said when referring to the ships and the port in general.

When one of these sludge tankers passed us on the river one morning, the smell of sewage that briefly came across the water was quite strong. An elderly, respectable type looking woman that had been watching the tanker go by, turned to Jerry standing on one side of her and said in a 'posh', high pitched, disgusted type voice, ' good grief! What on earth is that dreadful smell?

Jerry, with a half smoked rolled up cigarette perched on top of one ear, just visible under his blue woollen hat, turned and replied, 'its the sludge tanker madam.' Showing nicotine stained teeth through his beard he went on, ' mind you, it gets worse when they do stock taking.' The woman looked quite bewildered by this explanation, looking back at the passing tanker and then back at Jerry who's face hadn't moved a muscle. Before she could enquire further, he picked the half smoked cigarette off of the top of his ear, stuck it in his mouth, and reaching for his matches in his pocket went on, 'It's worse after Christmas time madam and on Christmas day they don't go to sea at all and send the crew around from door to door issuing corks!' With that, he adjusted his hat and finally said, ' Good day to you madam.' and walked off leaving the poor woman more mystified than ever.

I remained with the Red Funnel ferries until the end of 1974 and decided the time was right to move on. All shipping work involves long and unsocial hours and now at the age of 36, I felt as though I had done my fair share of it and would look for something once again that would give me more time at home with my wife and children.

The Esso refinery at Fawley near Southampton was advertising for process operators in their shore installations and also on their Marine Terminal. My brother Donald, who was a Chief Operator with Esso at the time, put a good word in for me and with my nautical experience, I could be useful during the loading and discharging of oil tankers. My application was accepted and after a vigorous medical, went to their refinery school for five weeks where they literally threw an oil refinery at you and set exams each week to ensure that some of it stuck. Having gone through the complexities of learning about pumps, drivers, compressors, fractionation, distillation and procedures dealing with all petroleum products, I was ready to take up the job on the Marine Terminal as an Operator.

There were nine tanker berths and I would spend a week on each berth, sketching, writing and learning about every pipeline, valve and control room, including all the safety regulations that goes with it, before moving on to the next. Once the training was over and you were allocated to a berth, the responsibility of loading and discharging of petroleum products was all yours.

Super tankers as they were known, would arrive and leave within 24 hours, using the tide to their full advantage to discharge their cargos. After berthing on a rising tide, they would be 'hosed up' and commence discharging crude oil at between, 8 000 tons to 10 000 tons per hour. Approximately eight hours later they would have discharged enough oil to prevent the vessel sitting almost on the bottom at low tide. This was a well practiced operation and when those pumps were put into operation, the roar and vibration caused by the crude oil gushing through the pipe lines, left the sole operator on the berth hoping they hadn't forgotten anything when setting the job up.

The work was interesting and extremely varied with all the different products requiring different loading and safety procedures. One such product was ethylene, which had to be around minus 30 degrees to remain in a liquid form and if it went up the scale too much it would turn to vapour. This would happen especially if the vessel loading the cargo had not had her temperatures brought down enough in the first place, leaving the berth operator having to recycle the gases. Those gases would then be sent back inshore by compressors and chilled down again in order for the ethylene to be returned to it's liquid state. This operation would take days in some cases and the ship owners wouldn't like it, but very often it would be their own fault by in trying to get the ship alongside and loaded when her tanks hadn't been chilled down enough to accept the product.

Regular visitors to the Marine Terminal were ' bunkering' tankers, which refuelled ships at anchor and also took various cargos around the South Coast including central heating oil, petrol and kerosene. Ship's fuel is known as ' bunkers ', probably from the days when all vessels were coal burners and the coal was kept in bunkers. I got to know the crew's quite well from their regular visits to the refinery and on one occasion, was offered a job as mate on one of their tankers.

The sea was still in my blood and here we go again I thought, knowing full well that I would be giving up a good paying job with many fringe benefits and an excellent pension scheme at the end of it all. After two years with the Esso refinery I decided I'd had enough and welcomed the change although there was a similarity in the type of work when loading and discharging cargos.

I became a skipper on these ships and with just a small crew onboard it was like one big happy family, all of us ' mucking in ' together when working on deck. We had a lot of fun and as we catered for ourselves, I used to do quite a bit of the cooking, as it's always been one of my favourite hobbies. Some of what we cooked came from the end of a fishing line when at anchor waiting for a berth, or usually when bunkering a ship. It was normal practice in those days for the skipper on the bunker vessel to get a bottle of whisky or similar, after refuelling and also something for the ships galley. All of these ' perks ' saved us a lot of money and we never had any guilt feelings about receiving such ' goodies ' as there were many occasions when we deserved something for our efforts. Clambering up rope ladders hanging over ship's sides, and rigging up hoses and derricks in the dead of night in freezing and foul weather conditions deserved a bottle of something to keep the circulation going.

With many of the big liners now gone from Southampton, many of the seamen appeared to have disappeared from our regular haunts around the port. I hadn't seen ' Froggy ' for several years and one morning I suddenly bumped into him down at our local paper shop and he was much the same as when I last saw him. His sea career had taken him on many cruises on Cunard Lines *Caronia,* which was known by many as the ' Green Goddess,' the ship being many shades of pastel green.

It was great to meet him again with his wife, both of them working for Southern Television in Southampton, himself being in the film cutting department, and his wife as a Vision Mixer. They took my kids down to the television station on several occasions to see children's programs being recorded, and the many attractions and props that were to be found in a busy television studio. A favourite at that time was a children's program called ' Runaround' which was hosted by Mike Reid, who may be better remembered as Frank Butcher in the BBC soap, East Enders.

Froggy and his wife owned a big black dog of which I can only describe as a Rogue Labrador, as unlike that particular breed, it was a bit aggressive now and then despite Froggy's wife saying the animal was only playing. It would nip my kid's rear ends when leaving their house and was akin to gnawing my hand when trying to placate the thing. If all of this was playtime to the animal, I wouldn't like to think what it would be like if the mutt got serious! There were times when I must have evened up the score with my little Jack Russell who would 'nip' his wife when she became over possessive with him or tried to pick him up when he just didn't want to be picked up.

Anyone that's owned a Jack Russell will know what I mean when I say they are lively little animals and in the case of my dog, extremely protective of its owner. My little 'Jacker ' was white with a black patch over each eye and a big black patch either side of his body. He had a docked tail of which I've never agreed with and a black patch underneath his tail in the shape of a bow tie, which looked like his rear end had been sewn up and was dressed for dinner. His proper name was Tim, but was better known as Timothy Tight Arse. One of Tim's drawbacks was his inability to do a clean 'job' and I would inevitably have to have some tissue handy to wipe him clean before allowing him back in the house.

One lunch time after taking the dogs for a walk, Froggy and I ended up in 'The Ark' public house and consumed thereafter, large quantities of a very strong brew known as ' Old English Ale ' On arrival at his house, Tim decided to christen Froggy's front lawn by crouching over and doing a 'job' and afterwards, scratching up the grass in order to cover up his droppings. As I made an attempt to wipe his backside, Froggy opened his front door causing the dog to dart through his legs, and in an attempt to stop him, pushed the animal over to one side in his hall way. Before we could stop him, the dog had left his calling card in the shape of a long skid mark on his wallpaper. Froggy, a little the worse for drink, but never ever losing his sense of humour shouted out, ' nice one Tim! Now go outside and have another crap and do it again to match the other side up!' It would be an understatement to say that his wife was not amused and ultimately, Tim was barred from his house for life and Froggy from the pub.

Events taking place at this time was the unexpected outcome of Southampton winning the F.A. Cup Final against Manchester United on May 1 in 1976, beating them 1-0, a real shock to many foot balling fans as Southampton was only a second division side at that time. The town of Southampton celebrated like never before and many observers reckoned it was a greater turn out than when World War 2 had ended. The kids in our neighbourhood went mad of course, standing outside of their front doors bedecked in the football club's colours, waving and cheering as their hero's went by on an open top double-decker bus. It's times like these that will be stamped on one's memory forever and it's a pity that there aren't more of these occasions to celebrate.

In 1977, my mother and father celebrated their Diamond Wedding anniversary at Rhinefield House in the heart of the New Forest. Rhinefield House was a beautiful stately home and although privately owned, part of it could be hired out for special occasions. It was a grand occasion with all the family and relations as far a field as Australia, attending the function, dining in medieval style with jugs of mead and glasses of wine being brought by serving wenches in front of roaring log fires.

It was a celebration worthy of a couple of whom had been married for 60 years, had ten children and had travelled the world together. It was an unforgettable evening with the press running the story and mentioning of course, my mother's connection with the *Titanic* disaster. A tree was planted for them at the flats where they lived and a party was held for all the residents, along with the Lord Mayor of Southampton attending.

In November of 1978, just five months after their anniversary, my father aged 83, passed away suffering from a stroke. My mother was devastated having lost her partner of 60 years and would now face those remaining years left to her, on her own. She had always been a strong willed woman and would remain physically independent for as long as possible, only requiring from her family those very important regular visits.

It always seems to be the case that when there is sadness or a run of bad luck, something always crops up to compound the problem. Whilst working in my garden building a wall. I overdid it one afternoon and ended up with a slipped disc. As a result of this problem, I was laid up for well over three months and once back at work, found my confidence had gone when undertaking simple tasks like climbing rope ladders or any type of heavy lifting. There was never any pressure on me to leave but I decided that if I couldn't do what I used to do, then it was time to move on and give someone else the job. I was now coming up to almost forty years of age and after nearly 25 years, of working on ship's, my seagoing days were finally over. I left the company in 1979 and became a taxi driver for a year in the hope that the light duties would help my back problem to recover. During this time we had moved into a newer more expensive property and of course a bigger mortgage to go with it, so the real challenge at this time was how to hang on to this extra burden without having any skills other than seamanship.

In order to try an earn a better wage to keep our mortgage payments up, I took on the job as a Pipe Fitters Mate now that my disc appeared to have stabilized, and worked on a revamped gas plant for almost a year. In the construction business, found the attitude of the workers quite similar to that of seamen, perhaps because their working lives involved moving from one job to the next with a change of scenery on a regular basis.

Once the job had come to an end on the site, we were all made redundant and the writing was now on the wall, I would have to learn to do something else. It was becoming imperative that I take up useful long term, employment again, so I decided to take up a Government Training course, as an Electrical Fitter at Southampton's training establishment in the Western Docks. This was a condensed course of six months duration and unless you were prepared to do homework as well, you would miss out on quite a bit, especially on the theoretical side of things. I had my own little desk set up at home in our bedroom and would pore over electrical theory in the hope of understanding something of which I knew absolutely nothing about. I got through it all finally, and was eventually offered a job in May of 1982 with Pirelli Telecom as a Tester at their Eastleigh plant.

Cable factories are usually designed as very long buildings and walking through the full length of that factory on my first day at work I wondered how long it would be before I started looking for another job. The noise of the machinery and the smell of the place didn't stir up much enthusiasm in me on that first day but I knew I had little choice so I would have to grin and bear it and give it a 'go.' I therefore decided that all things being considered, I would throw myself into my newfound occupation and do my best in getting on top of the job. My training in the testing of all types of copper conductors was, to say the least interesting, and I soon became engrossed in my work. I never thought it possible that I would learn to do such things as testing cables for cross talk, insertion loss, impedance, insulation resistance, mutual capacitance, attenuation, conductor resistance and high voltage tests. I mention this to mainly emphasise the irony of my being trained as an Electrical Fitter for six months, and then ending up doing something completely different.

Since leaving the sea, my life style had changed quite a bit, losing contact with many of my old shipmates and making new friends ashore. Within the last few years we had seen the death of one of my nephews aged just six years of age, again from leukaemia leaving us all wondering if this disease may be in the genes of our family. Up until the present time, there has never been any evidence to that effect and perhaps in the not too distant future, we may find out more about this terrible disease.

In December of 1980, we were also to hear of the death of my eldest brother Fred who had died from heart disease in London aged 62 and who's wish was to be cremated and have his ashes scattered on the Approaches to Southampton Water. He had worked as an anaesthetist in St Thomase's Hospital in London, and the heart surgeon that had operated on him was also his friend, explaining to my parents at his funeral, that he could do little to save him despite his efforts. In the early ' eighties ' we were to learn of the deaths of John Lennon and Steve McQueen and also the emergence of the Gulf War and the Battle of the Falklands.

After about three years of training at the Pirelli Cable factory, there was a revolution about to happen in the manufacture of telecommunications cable generally. At that time we were a busy factory, turning out on average 30 000 loop kilometres of cable per week, mostly just for British Telecom. Loop kilometres are measured in 1000 metre lengths whereby a cable with 20 conductors is known as being of 20 loop kilometres. With the introduction of fibre optic cable, testing techniques were quite different and involved the use of power metres, laser light sources, oscilloscopes, optical time domain reflectometers and a great deal of computer assistance. This all meant that one person could do the job of three or four people, and one fibre optic cable could do the same job and last longer, than a thousand copper conductors which meant that eventually, there would be many job losses.

During the early ' eighties ' there were a few press reports about proposed searches in the North Atlantic for the wreck of the *Titanic* and in 1984, plans were being made to do a proper ' sweep ' of the ocean floor in an area where the wreck was thought to be. On one of my regular Saturday morning visits to my mother I told her about the news items I had read and her exact words at the time were, ' they'll never find it. She's gone forever.' Whenever I think of those words, I have always had the feeling that my mother was saying that more in hope, than anything else. The *Titanic* story had always held my interest from as far back as my early teens and I would follow up on any news item relating to that ship whenever I could.

I would listen intently when my mother told us those stories of her and her parents when onboard that ship and of the many people they spoke to during the voyage. I would try to imagine how she must have felt watching that great liner sinking before her very eyes as she watched helplessly a short distance away from her lifeboat. She knew her father was out there somewhere, probably fighting for his life along with the rest of them and there was nothing any of them could do about it. She always ended her stories of the *Titanic* with the same far away look and sadness saying, ' I shall never forget those terrifying sounds when the ship went down and the screams and cries for help from those hundreds of people echoing across the water that night. It was absolutely dreadful.'

In 1985, there was much speculation in press reports about the possibility of raising the *Titanic* and the moral issues involved. The French and American scientists involved, were using the latest equipment and the general feeling was that it would be only a matter of time before the wreck was discovered. The handful of survivors left and relatives of the deceased, looked upon the wreck site, wherever it may have been, as the resting place of their loved ones.

During the first part of July 1985, a French research vessel, the *Le Suroit*, started a search in the area where it was thought the *Titanic* had gone down and by August, the U.S. Navy ship, *Knorr* had joined in the search. On September 1, at around 2 am, the underwater equipment of the *Knorr*, picked up an echo, which soon after, was revealed to be that of a ships boiler casing. A quick check on the *Titanic's* boiler room details from a Harland and Wolff manual showed that this was without doubt, a boiler from the stricken liner.

After a great deal of jubilation onboard of the research vessel after this discovery, it was decided by those onboard to observe a few minutes silence for those 1 500 souls that had perished at this place around 2 am, this being the same time as the finding of the boiler casing.

After 73 years the *Titanic* had finally been found in 13 000 feet of water, lying in darkness and at peace.

When reading about this discovery, I went to see my mother to tell her about this latest piece of news. When I arrived at her flat, she was sitting in her favourite armchair, dozing in front of the television. After letting myself in, I sat down opposite her and said somewhat excitedly, ' guess what mother? They've found the *Titanic*! '

Her look was one of utter amazement and then almost as though she didn't quite understand what I was saying replied, ' what do you mean? ' As she was hard of hearing, I said a little louder, ' The Americans have found the wreck of the *Titanic*. ' This time with a look of utter surprise on her face, she then said, ' what on earth are they going to do with it?' My reply to her, the tone of my voice suggesting that it all looked hopeless anyway was, ' I should think it's far too deep for them to do anything with mother.' Her reply had the ring of finality about it when she said, ' that's good then. The dead should be left in peace. '

Unfortunately, that was not to be, as the finding of the wreck would now begin to stir up ideas on those who could see many financial advantages coming out of the discovery. The quiet life my mother had enjoyed over the last few years was about to be changed dramatically as some people began to view her with renewed interest. Gone were those little chats from time to time with friends and relatives about the *Titanic*, now they wanted her autograph and more and more people were seeking her out to sign scraps of paper or anything else that came to hand.

Interviews followed and they would always want to know how she felt at the time of the ship striking the iceberg. Her replies were very good for her age and her memories had never faltered throughout her lifetime regarding that night. She would tell them that they were awakened when the ship struck the iceberg by a shuddering sensation, followed by the rattling of glass from the washstand and several bumps reverberating around the cabin. Her father had entered their cabin soon after and had helped her and her mother on with their life jackets before escorting them to the boat deck.

On going to the boat deck, they noticed a few passengers moving about the accommodation apparently unconcerned, before going upstairs and passing others, on their way down that had already braved the cold night air and were returning to their cabins. She would go on to tell her interviewers that at the age of fifteen, the thought of drowning never entered her head. When on the boat deck she distinctly remembers pointing out to her parents, lights on the horizon that must have belonged to a ship. Realising by this time that the *Titanic* could be in serious trouble, she found the sight of those lights to be comforting and felt that they would bring about their rescue. She would go on to say that shortly after pointing out those lights to her parents and the Rev. Carter, who was with them at the time, how the lights were suddenly turned off. Throughout this time she could always recall hearing the ship's orchestra playing lively music and tunes that were popular at that time.

Whenever my mother told me about that incident, I would ask her if she thought that she might have been mistaken, as very often on such a clear night at sea, stars can be seen almost on the horizon. She would always say with conviction that those lights they saw from high up on the *Titanic's* boat deck were brighter than the stars and for them to suddenly disappear like they did, proves they were ship's lights. I know from my own experience as a Lookout Man that on several occasions, I have reported the odd star or two just above the horizon. They could easily be mistaken for a ship's masthead lights and then a short time later, notice that the same 'lights' had become airborne due to the earth's rotation. This would be a standing joke amongst Lookout Men when being relieved from the watch to mention to each other that another ship ' has just took off and become airborne ' during their watch.

If it was a ship they all saw, then the turning out of the lights, as my mother described it, may well have been a vessel changing course away from the *Titanic,* causing the disappearance of the masthead lights and perhaps revealing a poor stern light, not seen from that distance. It has been documented that a Norwegian Sealer was in the vicinity at the time, indulging in illegal fishing and may well have seen the *Titanic's* rockets and decided to vacate the area for fear of detection. It has also been documented that the lights seen may well have been those of the Leyland freighter *Californian* which apparently was 'hove to ' in the area because of ice, but even to this day it has always been a controversial subject.

As a matter of interest from that time to the present day, ships over a certain length must display two masthead lights. The foremast light being lower than the after mast or mainmast light, giving an oncoming vessel a clearer indication of it's direction, other than relying on it's red and green port and starboard side lights.

During interviews, my mother always remembered people, bringing ice up on deck and throwing it about, laughing and saying the ship was unsinkable. She would always mention how fascinated she was to see this going on with the ship stopped in mid ocean and how this particular behaviour made people feel more at ease with the situation. As this went on, her father remained serious and continued to quietly puff on his cigar, appearing to realise more so than many others, the seriousness of the predicament they were now finding themselves in.

As the ship's orchestra continued to play lively music up on the boat deck, my mother always remembered her father being handed a glass of brandy from the Rev. Carter when he had reappeared up on the deck. When the time came for them to get into their lifeboat, Lillian, the Reverend Carter's wife was no longer with them and it was assumed that she had gotten into another boat further along the boat deck.

My mother would refer to the Carter's many times during interviews as they were their dining companions and also became very good friends during the voyage. She would always recall how her parents referred to them as a very religious devoted couple and how well her father and Earnest Carter got on together. It would mystify her as to why Lillian Carter later, was listed as drowned along with her husband as it's almost certain that he would have made sure that Lillian would have gotten into a boat. One theory was that if that were the case, she may well have climbed back out of the boat to be with her husband at the end, but it's highly unlikely that the boat's crew would have allowed her to get out once in the boat. It's also unlikely for her to have drowned if she had remained in the boat so the whereabouts of Lillian Carter on that night will no doubt forever remain a mystery.

There were many obscure press reports about the disaster with typical instances of passengers and crew alike being interviewed although still suffering from stress and trauma after many of them had lost loved ones. In my mother's particular case on arrival in New York, after leaving their rescue ship the *Carpathia*, they were hounded by the press everywhere they went and her mother, very often told them anything just to get rid of them.

They were both themselves feeling extreme grief after losing Thomas, a loving father and husband and were not in any state to receive a barrage of questions from reporters. At other times when the press followed them all over the place when shopping etc. they would shut themselves away in a lady's lavatory somewhere just to get rid of them. This was not to say that both women didn't realise the great help that they had received when in New York, had come about mainly as a result of the press but at that time, they wanted more than anything, just to be left alone. For the first few days after arrival on New York they were taken to various hospitals in the hope that Thomas had been found but it was the same story everywhere. Those that were connected with the sinking of the *Titanic* had either been discharged or had arrived with the rest of them on the *Carpathia*.

During the ever increasing public interest now being shown towards my mother, it was decided that she be protected from those that were out to see what they could get from her as there had been times when she would answer the door to complete strangers. There were many family collectables like, menu's, ceremonial swords and other items of interest that have gone missing over the years and it's been difficult to pin down who may have been around when these losses occurred. Now that my father was no longer with her she was becoming more vulnerable so we decided that she would answer the door to no one and each of us would have her for the weekends and during the week, we would take turns in calling on her daily. This was the only arrangement that she would agree to as she continued to insist on her independence.

In August of 1985 we were to learn of the death of my brother John, the sixth child born to my parents, who up until he was diagnosed as having cancer, had always led an extremely healthy life. He was 56 years of age and was a man greatly respected by everyone who knew him and his death came as a great shock to family and friends alike.

Having relatives in Australia I decided to give my kids a holiday of a lifetime and take them out there to meet cousins and family they had never met before. Andrew my son, elected to remain behind because of his job so I took both girls, Janina and Janette and we had a wonderful five weeks holiday, Janette forever saying that she wanted to stay. On our return and me back at work, life appeared to be going along quite well up to this point in this time and I would look back in amazement, to find that after nearly nine years, I was still in the same job and was by this time a Senior Test Technician. As far as I was concerned, I was made for life with all the fringe benefits that came with being on the staff, and a good pension to look forward to on retirement. Now that I was settled in a job I couldn't see what else could go wrong to change it, but life is full of surprises, and change it did. My marriage had run out of steam after 20 years and we decided to go our own ways and got divorced, although we have remained good friends to this very day. After the divorce, we sold up our home and me and the kids, moved to Midanbury, a suburb of Southampton.

We were ' ripped off ' when buying this home but there was pressure on me to sell after the marriage had wound up. I should have taken the previous owners to court for breach of contract, but we decided to get stuck in and save ourselves a lot of bother of which we just didn't have time for. With the help of my son Andrew who was now working, my two daughters, and some friends, we cleared the garden out which the previous owners should have done, and we also redecorated the house, making the place a bit more respectable. When first moving into this place you could say it looked like the type of home that had to be decorated before it could be condemned, but we were desperate and it was our fault for accepting it in the first place.

April 15, 1987, saw the 75th anniversary of the sinking of the *Titanic* and there were many press reports regarding the raising of the vessel and again survivors were saying that the wreck should be left alone. My mother never liked the idea of the ship being disturbed, and asked me to write a letter for her to find out what the salvage companies intentions were. At the beginning of September, I decided to write to the historian of the *Titanic Historical Society* in California who wrote the text of the historical illustrated volume, ' *Titanic,* ' in 1992. He had always kept in close touch with my mother, long before the wreck was discovered and was a genuine enthusiast with a wide range of knowledge on the subject. I thought that if anyone knew what was going on, he would probably be the best one to contact.

In my letter, I stressed my mother's concerns, not so much about the ship itself but more so about personal belongings that may be retrieved from the wreck. His reply was sympathetic stating how much public support had gone against the French for participating in the salvage effort and also, if they had known before hand, they would never have taken part in the project. He also went on to say that to the best of his knowledge at that time, artefacts recovered would not be sold but would be displayed in a museum. He also mentioned in his letter, the feelings of another survivor, who had been one of the most vociferous in denouncing the expedition, along with the majority of other survivors. He ended his letter by saying that he hoped that those items recovered would be positively identified and claimed by relatives, but doubted if that would be outcome. The 75th anniversary of the sinking of the *Titanic* also saw my mother flying out to America with other survivors, which was organised by the Historical *Titanic* Convention.

As the decade was drawing to a close, I decided to put my house up for sale as the housing market had become extremely attractive with people being handed mortgages on a plate and would buy anything to get into the housing market. Property prices were going through the roof at that time and houses were being sold for ' silly money ' their values being pushed up on a monthly basis. We stayed in that house for just two years before moving out, making a good profit from the sale and moving into a far better home just down the road in Townhill Park, not far from where we used to live just 20 years previously.

We were happy there and everyone liked the place and once more we could settle and get a decent home together again. These were the Thatcher years and interest rates kept rising and people kept losing their jobs, unemployment became a way of life for many and we were saddled with the Poll Tax, Life goes on as they say, until the next time which turned out to be massive redundancies at the factory where I worked, leaving hardly anyone in the place, and most of the cable operations going to Wales. I was now 53 years of age and being made redundant posed a few problems, especially as the only other cable manufacturer in the region was a submarine cable division in the docks and they weren't taking on anyone.

With Australia now beginning to enter my thoughts on a regular basis, I decided to spend a bit of my redundancy money on a holiday to go on another trip out there, to visit my daughters who by this time had become permanent residents. My son Andrew, who had already done his share of back packing around Australia, was also channelling his thoughts in that direction. Finding a job was going to be a problem at my age so I put that on ' the back burner' until I came back as I didn't see the point in losing any sleep over it. It didn't take much figuring out one way or the other, when one realised that short of being a brain surgeon, or nuclear scientist, there wouldn't be much out there in the way of ' real jobs ' for people like me.

After leaving Pirelli's in 1991, I took up a temporary job as a Y.T.S. (Youth Training Scheme) Supervisor, a Government Training scheme to get young people off of the dole and working. My work involved taking small groups of teenagers to different areas and getting them employed in clearing away public footpaths and hedgerows etc. generally getting them ' work orientated ' Part of this work involved the Supervisor talking to these young people and relaying to them his or hers own various work experiences and for them in turn, to get across what they really wanted to do with their own lives. I would have to give a report on each one every month regarding behaviour, ability and the way they applied themselves to the tasks given to them, all of this on a point scoring system.

During our discussion periods there would be some enlightening replies to some of my questions, one of them wanting to be an undertaker because he liked working with people and another wanting to be an astronaut but was afraid of heights. No doubt they would have their bit of fun but there was some serious talks about their futures and I'm sure some of them appreciated what help I could offer. I was quite popular with them mainly because I wouldn't allow them to work in the rain whereas other Supervisors made their groups carry on regardless of foul weather, thinking it would toughen them up. I made my position clear from the onset to the Senior Supervisor, who was known as Hitler, that they weren't prisoners and if the local authority was prepared to issue the appropriate clothing, I too would let them work out in all weathers. He reminded me of the type of person who may well attend ban the bomb marches, enjoy home made lemonade or be the first in line to attend public hangings.

There were a few problems between them now and then and on one occasion, one lad was just about to chop another boy's head off with a scythe, as I quickly got between them just in time. Apart from the odd isolated incident, I felt sorry for these kids and gave them good marks every month when handing in their report sheets in order to help them out of a system that wasn't any of their making. I did this work for twelve months and it was doubtful if they had learnt anything about what direction to take, but it discounted them from the dole figures, which in my opinion, was what it was all about in the first place.

My next job was with Hampshire County Council, temporarily employed in the Highway's Department rating roads for future repairs. This was a good little ' number ' being given a car and a list of roads to look at each week, checking them for major and minor defects. I would park the car out in the beautiful Hampshire countryside and walk along the country lanes pushing a measuring wheel and recording the road conditions for every 100meter length. Unfortunately this was only a summer job, which lasted for about five months and then I was out of work until they sent for me again the following year. However, I'd had enough by this time and my mind was made up, I would apply to emigrate and join my daughters out in Australia.

Newspaper reports during the early nineties were coming out quite regularly with news of up to 2 000 artefacts having been taken from the wreck of the *Titanic*. One such news item in April 1991 revealed, that my mother would soon take part in an incredible reunion with these artefacts, which would soon go on show by a French team. There was to be three months of worldwide advertising and the issue of catalogues which would be shown to families, who may be able to identify some of the items. My mother was quite excited about this as she and her parents had travelled with a great deal of jewellery and gold sovereigns during the voyage and she particularly remembers leaving behind a gold and coral necklace on her bunk when vacating their cabin to go up to the boat deck. Apart from the valuable silverware, crockery and linens in the ships hold that her father had purchased in London in order to stock his new hotel in Seattle, my mother could never forget the gold pocket watch her father always wore in his waistcoat. He also had with him a Gladstone bag, which apparently held a considerable amount of bank notes, gold sovereigns and jewellery.

Among other *Titanic* news items in the papers in 1992, there was coverage of my mother aged 95, being reunited with two other ladies that had survived the disaster, Melvina Dean, aged 80, and Eva Hart, aged 87. This meeting was arranged for the opening of the exhibition, *Titanic Voices,* in Southampton's Maritime Museum. The ages of these survivors in 1912 were Miss Dean, a baby at just nine weeks, Eva Hart at seven years of age and my mother aged fifteen. Melvina Dean had a brother, Bertram who was also a survivor.

In 1993, a ceremony held at the Hilton Hotel in Southampton was arranged by the salvage company *R.M.S. Titanic inc.* My mother, at the age of 97, was presented with her father's gold pocket watch, which had been brought up from the wreck site. I can remember my mother telling us as children that one of her step brothers had always claimed that her father had promised him the watch in his will, and that it had the inscription on the back, TWS Brown. According to the stories our mother used to tell us, her father always wore his pocket watch in his waist coat and had it on him when standing on the boat deck that night as the ship went down. I can't remember any of my family ever seeing the back of the watch as it was face out in it's presentation box and seeing the watch myself, I noted that it was in remarkable condition so the engraving on the back should still be visible.

My application to migrate to Australia was being processed at this time and also at this time, I was to learn that my second eldest brother, Ken, was diagnosed as suffering from Alzheimers disease. He had always been a bachelor living on his own, and I would visit him on many occasions and take him to his local pub for a drink which he always looked forward to. I began to find out from neighbours that he would be wandering around at all hours of the day and night and it was clear that he was developing a short-term memory loss. I arranged for him to see a doctor and it was later confirmed that he had Alzheimers disease and would need to go into care. He was put into a home in Basingstoke and I took my mother up there to see him before leaving for Australia, and this was to be the last time they were ever to see each other again.

Australia House in London had notified me that my application to emigrate had been approved and I immediately put our house on the market. The Thatcher government had now created a housing slump with many repossessions taking place and houses being sold well below the prices and valuations of just two or three years ago. The last time we had our house up for sale the phone never stopped ringing but now, it was silent and I thought we were going to be held up for an indefinite period before leaving for Australia. After advertising extensively for some weeks, we finally had some luck whereas someone local, just a few streets away, had always wanted to move to where we were situated. I lost a lot of money on the sale, around something like, 20% of our original purchase price but considered our selves fortunate in being able to sell the house in the first place at this time. After sorting ourselves out, I flew from London's Heathrow Airport on September 26, 1994.

Then there was Ollie, one of our cooks,
Oily by name and oily by looks.
Using his hands instead of his tools,
He would be breaking all culinary rules.

Oil and sweat oozing, from out every pore,
You would be left, not wanting for more.
Watching him at work, never ever flustered,
Dishing up sweet, with a handful of custard.

Haisey.

The author and his wife Lyn with his grandfather's gold pocket watch brought up from the Titanic *wreck site.*

Chapter Six
Brisbane

It was good to be back in Brisbane, this time hopefully to settle and leave all my troubles behind me. I was met by my daughters, son in laws and grandchildren at the airport, and was quite amazed at the way the children had grown up since last seeing them all. We had a party that night at Janette's home in Sunnybank but half way through the evening, jet lag had taken over and I collapsed until late the next day. I was to start all over again from scratch and as always the first priority was to look for work. It would be different this time, as I would have to live off of my own money, my emigration category not allowing for the safety net of unemployment benefit, if unable to find work, which in turn meant living on a tight budget.

I had two jobs to start with but only of short duration, one as a pawn brokers assistant which would have been more suitable for a school leaver and the other, working in a pine furniture factory which was temporary, and appeared to be full of young people and school leavers. I applied for many jobs and attended more interviews in a year, than I ever did in England in a lifetime but all to no avail, my past skills apparently were not recognised by the powers to be, and when they were, my age was against me anyway.

Once again I would have to try something entirely different, and pursue employment where my age would not be so much of a drawback. I started training as a security officer in the hope that I may have a job that I could settle into. Unfortunately, once the training was over the job prospects weren't much better unless I had undertaken additional training in first aid or went for training to carry a gun, and perhaps further training to do security work for industrial sites or hospital work. I couldn't afford to pay for anymore training courses and after nine months and all my savings practically gone, I began to fear the worst when at long last, one of my applications bore fruit. I was taken on as a school cleaner, a new experience for me but for the time being, this would have to do to ' keep the wolves from the door' until something else turned up.

My future wife to be Lyn, arrived after almost a year of waiting for her application to be processed and that in itself was making life difficult for us both, not being together and forever trying to plan a future by phone calls and letters. As luck would have it, after she had arrived there was another job vacancy at the school and we managed to get a job for her as a cleaner there as well. Much to our surprise, we settled into this type of work and found the school to be a good employer and we were left pretty much alone to get on with the job in hand. After several weeks, we began to find that things weren't so bad and at our ages, we had to take what was on offer anyway, and get on with it   We found the work to be well paid when combining our wages, and we also had more leisure time on our hands than ever before, so things weren't quite so bad as first thought.

By August of 1995, I had heard from relatives and friends overseas, that our mother had become quite immobile by this time and was taken everywhere by wheelchair, forever signing autographs on bits of paper or whatever came to hand. It was during this period that she had received an invitation from the American salvage group, *R.M.S. Titanic,* to go on a short cruise of remembrance to the *Titanic* wreck site. Some of the reports we had heard here in Australia were telling us that our mother was now attending functions all over the place and had a publicity agent and private nurse to help her along with her strenuous schedule. We were told that she was now very frail and people were expressing their views about leaving her to live out the final years of her life in peace. She was now, 99 years of age and would fly out to America to go on this short cruise to the wreck site to pay her last respects to her dear father, something she had always wanted to do throughout her life.

Before undertaking this voyage, she was to hear of the death of her fourth son, Kenneth, who had passed away from Alzheimers disease at 75 years of age. With my father passing away from a stroke back in 1976, she had now outlived 5 members of her family. On arrival in New York, she boarded the 31 000 ton cruise ship *Island Breeze* along with a few other remaining survivors and a ship full of sightseers and people involved with publicity, exhibitions and the salvage operations. At this time another cruise ship was also chartered with sightseers and it had been arranged by the salvagers for a huge chunk of the *Titanic's* hull to be brought to the surface in what was to be another publicity ' spectacular.' Unfortunately for those waiting in anticipation of seeing a large piece of the *Titanic* being raised from the depths, they were to be disappointed, as it had to be released before reaching the surface due to bad weather conditions prior to this event.

On arrival at the wreck site, 310 nautical miles south of Newfoundland at a position, 41 46'N 50 14' W, the *Island Breeze* stopped, below them lay the wreck of the *Titanic* at a depth of 13 000 feet, in darkness and at peace. For the North Atlantic, the weather could only be described as superb for the ceremony that took place and the service which followed, was accompanied by a lone piper playing a lament on his pipes. The hymns and prayers were held on the open deck in a very moving ceremony for those 1 500 souls that had perished at this place 84 years ago. After the service, my mother was wheeled to the ship's rail in her wheelchair and peering over the side, let a wreath fall onto the dark waters below in memory of her dear father. My mother was deeply moved and wept silently, as the memories of that fateful night came flooding back to her as her father along with 1 500 other souls must have fought for their lives in those icy waters. She had finally carried out her life long desire to pay her last respects to her father and at 99 years of age, had finally achieved that.

On returning to England after this cruise, preparations were being made for her 100th birthday celebrations on October 27, which were to be held at the Hilton Hotel in Southampton.

As I settled down in my home in Sunnybank, I found that I had quite a bit of time to myself and decided to take up one of my once favourite hobbies of drawing and painting. This was my best subject at school, mainly when in art classes, I was usually left alone to get on with what I was doing which suited me fine. My favourite subjects for sketching and painting were ships of course, and I would become completely absorbed in my efforts, feeling that I was actually there, building the subject with every line of my pencil or stroke of my brush. I found that although much older these days and picking up again on something I hadn't done in years, I still had that feeling of creating something from nothing and to me, the recapturing of my imagination, was what inspired me to give it another go.

All of my paintings are mostly from memory and to copy something, never gives me that complete challenge or satisfaction that I so enjoy when I first start sketching from scratch. I decided at this time that I would undertake creating a picture gallery of my own of all the ships that I had served on throughout my life and I knew when I started this task it would take time, but it's something I always wanted to do and hope to complete it when I've retired.

I had started painting pictures of the *Titanic* by this time and this generated a bit of interest from people who were enthusiastic about the subject. My first priority was to get a painting together for each member of my family with my mother's signature to ensure that my children would have something to remember their grandmother by.

Between my painting and sketching sessions, and trips out with my daughters and their families, a friend of mine, Malcolm, who had emigrated several years before me, had purchased a 40 acre block of land, some 50 miles from Brisbane, as a long term investment. It was a joint ownership arrangement between us, splitting it fifty- fifty in the hope that one day we could make some money out of it for our old age. This land was reasonably well situated, with a good view for many miles around and was on sloping ground. We went out there several times and were never short of ideas of what we could do on this piece of land but unfortunately, we finally sold it for roughly the same as we paid for it three years previously. Today, we have a feeling that we may have regretted that decision and I don't think we would want to go out there again to see what may have developed, as I'm sure if we had stayed with it, we could have done quite well out of it.

In August of 1996, I suppose I was as shocked as everyone else to learn of the death of Princess Diana and as with President Kennedy, you knew what you were doing at the time of hearing the news. People of prominence get such a wide range of media coverage that when something like this happens, you feel as if you knew them personally and as a result, the news has quite an impact. By December of this year, I had married my second wife Lyn at my daughter's house in Sunnybank Hills with the service being held in her garden, which was for us both, a wedding with a difference.

Continuing news from overseas, regarding the repeated dives on the *Titanic* wreck site, involved press reports that were far from kind to the operations going on in the North Atlantic. There were quotes of ' grave robbers', and references to the cruises over the site as that of ' a circus ' and another quote saying that this was ' dishonouring the memory of those that had died. ' A respected researcher involved with the discovery of the *Titanic* had said on video, with words to the effect, that the retrieval of personal items from the wreck was no different than going through the baggage of the dead from a crashed airliner.

Having received our official invitations we made preparations for the flight to London to attend my mother's 100th birthday celebrations. After arriving at

London's Heathrow Airport, my wife and I journeyed down to the Southampton Hilton Hotel for my mother's birthday celebrations. We were jet lagged when we arrived but were determined to make this a night to remember for our mother and the rest of our remaining family. On meeting her in her hotel room, she appeared tired, but quite well and having just finished dressing for the evening celebrations, was helped into her wheelchair. Before dinner that evening there were many photo calls and apart from her being surrounded by so many people and appearing somewhat bewildered by it all, there was a never ending stream of people repeatedly getting her to sign autographs and then finally walking away clutching hand's full of bits of paper with her signature on them. These people weren't enthusiasts but were there merely to see what they could get out of the evening for their own personal gain, and none of the organisers making any effort to stop it.

Some of the guests invited included, Melvina Dean a survivor, the President of *R.M.S. Titanic inc.* Senora E. Marconi, daughter of Sr. Guglielmo Marconi the

My mother, at her one-hundredth birthday celebrations, being presented with a bou-quet of flowers from George Tulloch, owner of the salvage company, Titanic Inc.

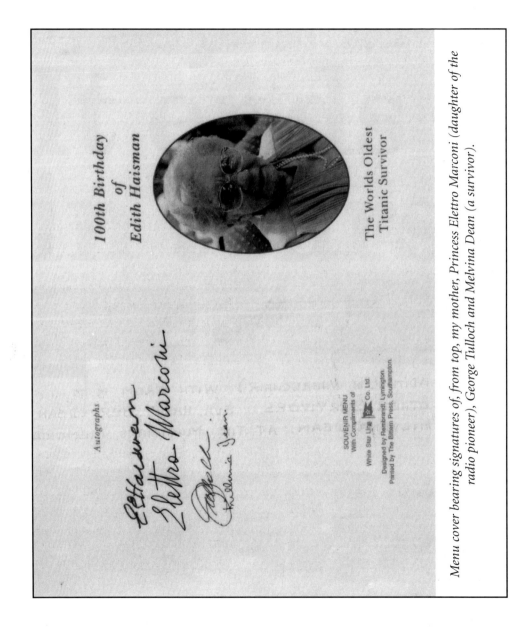

Autographs

100th Birthday
of
Edith Haisman

The Worlds Oldest
Titanic Survivor

SOUVENIR MENU
With Compliments of
White Star Line Co. Ltd

Designed by Rembrandt, Lymington.
Printed By The Bittern Press, Southampton.

Menu cover bearing signatures of, from top, my mother, Princess Elettro Marconi (daughter of the radio pioneer), George Tulloch and Melvina Dean (a survivor).

radio pioneer, and William MacQuitty, producer of the film, 'A Night To Remember '

Champagne had been produced for the 100th birthday celebrations, with a picture of my mother on the bottle, under the White Star Line logo. It was a fitting tribute to her and although tired, I'm sure she enjoyed the evening held in her honour.

My wife and I flew up to Scotland the next day to attend the wedding of Lyn's son from her first marriage, which was carried out in the finest Scottish tradition of kilts, bag pipes and enough whisky to drown the lot of us before returning to Southampton to finish off our holiday. I visited my mother in a nursing home in Portswood, Southampton, for the last time before leaving for Australia and she looked tired and very frail, both of us I think, knowing that we would never see each other again. Before leaving, one of the nursing staff came up to my mother and said, ' have you enjoyed having your visitors today Mrs Haisman?' Smiling, and then politely in a weak voice she replied, ' yes thank you.' and then, always proud of her kids went on, ' he's my youngest you know.'

At 7.30pm, January 20, 1997, just two months after we had arrived back in Brisbane, my mother passed away quietly in her sleep after suffering from pneumonia, this being her 101st.year. She had left behind four sons, two daughters and 40 grandchildren after outliving four of her own children and husband, and was finally laid to rest with my father and brother Brian, at St. Mary's Extra Cemetery in Sholing, Southampton.

Shortly after my mother's death there were press reports about the new *Titanic* movie being made by 20th Century Fox on a set that had been constructed in Baja California, Mexico. A full size model of the ship had been built which showed just one side only and apparently during filming, the filming sequences would be reversed to reveal the other non -existent side when required. It was feared that the whole project, which was approaching the 100 million dollar budget may well go over that figure and the building of only 'half a ship' was decided on to keep costs down. *Titanic* enthusiasts from various societies that had the privilege of visiting the set were greatly impressed by the authenticity of it all and were particularly impressed by the reconstruction of the grand staircase.

When the movie had it's premier in Brisbane, 20th Century Fox, invited me, my brother and sister to attend the first showing at the theatre in Brisbane's Queen Street Mall. Prior to the viewing we had the press and television reporters around during the afternoon at my sister's house before going into the city for the evening showing of the film. It was a pleasant evening with several family and friends there and we had a few complimentary drinks before going into the cinema to watch the latest of all *Titanic* epics. My personal opinion of the movie itself was that it had been very entertaining and the special effects used for the film were impressive. It has brought to many people the events that took place that night and although a story that will never go away, I think this movie has stirred up renewed interest throughout the world about the *Titanic* story.

I had sailed many times from Southampton's Ocean Terminal on the Cunard White Star Liners during my seagoing days and the set that showed the *Titanic's* departure day on the movie, is very much how it was in my day and appeared quite realistic. There was even a shot which showed the South Western Hotel in the background and if someone stood at that spot today in Southampton's Eastern Docks they would get a similar view as that on the movie. For me, it was the odd scene like this that made the film interesting, and some of the shipboard

The author at his mother's street sign in Southampton.

My mother's birthday book, which she took in Lifeboat 14, leaving behind her gold and coral necklace.

scenes revealed that the producers of the film had done their homework on that aspect of the production.

I think this movie has enlightened many people about events back in 1912 who perhaps otherwise, would never have given the subject a second thought and it has certainly stirred up interest throughout the world about the *Titanic* story. After seeing the film, many of us gathered in the foyer afterwards and chatted about how much our mother would have enjoyed this epic had she still been alive.

At the beginning of 1997, it was put to me by my great niece Marise, and her husband Mario, that I should think about writing my mother's life story. It was a bit of a challenge especially, as I had never done anything like this before but I decided to give it some thought anyway. I began to mull over the project during the following weeks and became inspired from the realization that so much had taken place over the whole 100 years of her life, that there would be much to write about. She had lived through the Boer war in South Africa where she was born and then the *Titanic* disaster, followed by two world wars and the raising of ten children in England. I had some doubts as to whether I could give her life story the full justice it deserved, but came to the conclusion that her story should be written by one of her own family if at all possible. I decided to give it a go, bearing in mind that it would be a fitting tribute to our mother if written by one of her own children, giving it the feeling and personal, credible approach this kind of story needed.

The many stories she had told us when we were young reflected her upbringing, which was very upright and Victorian. We would laugh when she told us about slapping my father's face after he pulled her down to sit on to his knee at a social function after only just meeting him. We would listen with respect, at her beliefs in the after life and of her and her mother's extraordinary experience with a clairvoyant in Melbourne two years after the sinking of the *Titanic*. She had always maintained that the clairvoyant had contacted her father and had written his signature down on a piece of paper in front of their very eyes. My mother had kept this piece of paper for many years afterwards but had mislaid it during the war years although my sister Joy, had seen it and had confirmed that it was an exact replica of my grandfather's signature. My father on the other hand, would on the occasion, treat these little chats with a bit of fun saying, 'Edith. You must have dreamt it.' She would take it all in good humor and laughing, would say in return to us kids, ' Don't listen to your father, he doesn't know what he's talking about!'

She would tell us about her own father having, as she called it, 'second sight' and how he could for see impending disasters, as was the case with the *Titanic*, and from all of this, one can draw the conclusion that many other people from that era were that way inclined. It's well known that seamen in those days were superstitious and had considered the late sailing of the *Titanic* on her maiden voyage, as that of a bad omen. The near collision in the docks as the ship was leaving Southampton for Cherbourg was also considered to be a bad omen, again a bad sign for a ship about to set sail on her maiden voyage.

I personally, could never accept the mystique or the outcome of such beliefs, but I was always impressed by her sincerity, when revealing the story about her and her mother during their meeting with a clairvoyant in Melbourne. It was in the light of this that I decided to include this experience in her life story, irrespective to what I felt about such things. It was her life story that I was attempting to write, and all things being considered, I had made up my mind from the onset that it would be written the way she had told it to us over the years and the way I had understood it throughout my lifetime.

During 1998, my wife and I were blessed with four more grandchildren, although one of them William, of whom was born to my daughter Janette, had a poor start in life. For several months the child literally starved due to his continuing vomiting and his inability to keep food down. This naturally caused a great deal of concern for everyone around the family and the thought of leukemia striking again were thoughts we quickly tried to brush aside. After undergoing extensive tests in Brisbane Children's Hospital, he was finally diagnosed as having, S.C.I.D.S. (Severe Combined Immuno Deficiency Syndrome), a rare condition found in children.

These children were known as ' Bubble Babies ' just a few years ago and were kept in a sterile plastic type bubble environment, to prevent them from coming into contact with the every day germs and bacteria that normal people usually cope with. William underwent treatment in Sydney Children's hospital for bone marrow transplantation and further tests and surprised just about everyone involved by his good recovery. A short while after his bone marrow transplant he began to make good progress and started to produce cells, which would help in developing his own immunity. So successful has his treatment been that there was considerable publicity on his remarkable recovery, and this has led my daughter to write a book on William's experience titled, ' Surviving SCIDS '

Throughout this year, tremendous interest was being generated due to the showing of the movie *Titanic,* which was officially released in March, winning eleven Oscars. The number of *Titanic* ' experts ' on the internet, and the ' knowledge' from the many *Titanic* societies was mind boggling and seemed to spring up over night. I had an e- mail from one society telling me that they knew more about my mother than I did and what she was supposed to have said and what she didn't say back in 1912. Its all quite extraordinary stuff, mostly gleaned from obscure press reports at that time from newspaper reporters hell bent on interviewing survivors suffering from stress and trauma.   Many of these ' experts ' would have difficulty in knowing one end of a ship to the other and would never have a clue about what it would be like to be in an ice field or onboard a ship in conditions such as that experienced by the *Titanic's* crew and passengers.

However, there was much money to be made out of the *Titanic* story and stories mostly followed the same pattern by always quoting the rich and famous onboard although those particular passengers were in the minority and suffered far less than the rest.   It is perhaps as well to remember that of the hundreds of thousands of people carried across the North Atlantic at that time and that figure increasing years later, to millions, the loss of 1 500 looks insignificant by comparison. This shows a far better safety record than air travel worldwide. That is not to say that the *Titanic* disaster wasn't one of the worlds worst shipping disasters, but it does show that all modes of transport have had their disasters and having paid the price, have learned a great deal from those disasters.

I have served with seamen in the British Merchant Navy who have had relatives that had served on the *Titanic,* and had also spoken to Fred Fleet, *Titanic's* Lookout Man when he was a newspaper seller in Southampton. The general feeling was that everyone had done their best out of an impossible situation and Captain Smith must have cursed the British Board of Trade for not updating the life saving and lifeboat requirement for his ship at that time.

The Board of Trade was ' God ' to shipping companies and mariners alike, and as long as their out of date specifications for lifesaving at sea were adhered to, they would consider the vessel worthy of its passenger carrying capacity and issue the appropriate certificate to that end. Building these huge liners which were more than twice the size of anything afloat during that period, came about in a very short time leaving the Board of Trade too slow in updating requirements for this new breed of vessel. The decisions to issue certificates for seaworthiness and lifesaving capabilities would be completely out of the captain's hands and he would be expected to take his ship to sea. Refusal would have been unheard of at that time and had that been the case, it may well have meant his being replaced, demoted or even the loss of his job.

Towards the end of 1998, my book was ready for the publishers after no less than three rewrites but I should imagine that would be normal for many would be writers tackling their first book. I had no problem putting together the nautical side of things and much of the research started from my homeport of Southampton. The general flow of my mother's life story came through quite easily, much of it we had grown up with and also through our own family research. I found it useful having much older brothers and sisters as their recollections came from a period in my parent's lives when they would have been that much younger to recall their experiences. It was becoming apparent that the many stories flooding the bookshops after the release of the film had left the whole *Titanic* saga in a state of being totally ' flogged to death.'

In March 1999, my book was published and at long last, I would now find out about how much reaction there would be to my efforts. The response was quite favourable, although by this time the *Titanic* movie was beginning to run out of steam and interest was beginning to dwindle in many bookshops. Towards the end of March, Brisbane's Channel Nine ' Extra' program, had interviewed my sister and I at the end of that month, and the program on our mother's story was screened. We all thought the coverage was excellent and were well pleased with the dignified way the program portrayed our mother's life and her experience on the *Titanic*.

It was during this time that I sent a copy of my book to the South African Titanic Society who had picked up the story on the internet. This is of great interest to many in that country as my mother was South African by birth and was up until the time of her death, their only living survivor as I recall.

This was becoming a busy time for me with interviews on local radio stations and at public libraries around Brisbane along with several other functions that were being generated by *Titanic* enthusiasts. During April I had a phone call from one of the organisers of the *Titanic* exhibition that would soon be visiting Brisbane and my sister, wife and I were invited to lunch at a hotel for discussions on the sale of my book at the exhibition and our involvement for the opening night. It was arranged that I set up my own table at the venue and sell my books from there, with many of my mother's personal effects in glass cabinets and large portraits of her situated close by.

The exhibition was situated at Brisbane's South Bank and after a cocktail party in which my sister and I gave an opening speech, the doors were open to the public on Saturday May 1.   By this time, I was well into writing my second book but with work at the school and selling books at the exhibition, this went on the back burner for a spell. Although the sale of books went well as one would expect at this type of venue, I found the more interesting aspect at this type of function was talking to the public and answering their many questions. The movie had brought the story to many people for the first time and much of their questioning was a direct result of that, but without spoiling the image they had, I would always stress that the crew, were in my opinion, portrayed in a bad light.

I could never understand why this was so, nor many of my fellow seafarers but perhaps it was decided that it would make a better story line. The crew were shown as being incompetent and at times cowardly but there were passenger reports after the disaster that revealed how highly they thought of the crew 's professionalism and conduct on that night. When one considers that almost three quarters of the crew drowned that night and the remaining 25% did their utmost in trying to save the rest, the question of cowardice and incompetence just doesn't add up. It was well known that Captain Smith spent a great deal of time on the wing of the bridge with a loud hailer, calling out to boats to return to the sinking ship to pick up more survivors but this was never revealed by most story tellers. It may well be that those making enquiries that followed after the disaster were looking for scapegoats in those days and who better than the crew, who only had the Seamen's Union to represent them but precious little other consideration from any other quarter.

The question of some boats leaving the stricken liner without a full complement of survivors was understandable in some cases when one considers the angle of the sinking vessel during the later stages of it's sinking. When the height of the boat deck from the water is appreciated as the vessel is on an even keel, the falls (ropes) for lowering would have had ample length to ensure that the lifeboats could be lowered safely down to the water. As the ship's bow sank lower and the stern went higher, the drop from the after end of the boat deck to the water would have almost doubled, and many boats would have run out of rope long before reaching the water. One can imagine the disastrous results if that had happened, and this would have been another consideration for the *Titanic's* officers and crew in the short time they had available.

There was the question of lifeboat No 1 leaving with 12 persons onboard, and being what's commonly known at sea as an accident boat, it would have been smaller than the rest although it's capacity was, at least 35 persons when fully loaded. What went on in that boat after it got away from the ship is open to question. Sir Cosmo Duff Gordon and his entourage would have had quite an influence on the crew after offering each one of them a 5 pound promissory note, equal to a month's wages in those days. It was stated during one of the enquiries that he made this offer to the boat's crew as he felt sorry for them after losing all their kit on the sinking ship.

Questions put to me at the exhibition were wide and varied and at times, quite comical with many people asking me if my mother had survived the disaster. We had some fun on the odd moment although it was considered by the

Publicity photo of the author and Titanic *model at* Titanic *exhibition in Auckland, New Zealand.*
—Courtesy Auckland City Council

majority to be a solemn occasion and people were greatly affected by the story generally. There were those that were moved by the exhibition after reading the many stories by survivors, causing them to be easily brought to tears. Others were angry, accusing the captain of negligence and of mass murder, not really grasping what the situation was, and relying too heavily on the latest movie. It's well known amongst seafarers that the *Titanic* followed virtually the same procedures and routines as her sister ship the *Olympic* during her crossings, and the speed of the *Titanic* at the time of the collision was within the range of 22 to 23 knots. This was below her cruising speed of 24 knots and that of her main competitor, the Cunard liner *Mauretania.*

Although smaller, this was a ship of greater horsepower with a cruising speed of 25 knots, that speed being considered as acceptable to ship owners and their masters up until that time. It should also be considered that a huge ship like the *Titanic,* would take a day or two to settle down and with the good weather conditions during that voyage, those great reciprocating engines of hers would perform better each day without extra coal being fed to the boilers.

A popular question from many was, why did Captain Smith after receiving so many ice warnings, decide to put some of these messages from the radio shack into his pocket instead of having them sent to the officer of the watch on the bridge. As a professional, the captain would have read each message and would have known that many of those ice warnings were giving the same position of the massive ice field, as those already posted up on the bridge. Clearly he was aware of the danger, had lookouts doubled up and made a course alteration 15 minutes before the scheduled alteration at 6pm, known as ' turning the corner ' This alteration would take the ship some 16 nautical miles further south, avoiding the reported ice field and this was achieved successfully. The *Titanic* did not run into a massive ice field but struck one solitary iceberg further south than the reported ice mass.

After the first week at the exhibition, putting in several hours each day, it was decided that during the week we would give it a miss and only attend at the weekends, this being the busiest times. During the second week my wife, sister and I received an invitation as guests of honour at the Court Restaurant at Cleveland, a suburb of Brisbane. This was for dinner on two consecutive nights for two special *Titanic* evening, which included a concert. This was a fine evening and a great deal of thought went into it and the owners of that restaurant deserve credit for their efforts that night. Other functions and lectures continued throughout the exhibition period at Brisbane, which later, was extended for a further two weeks by public demand.

I was asked many questions about the ship itself and several people mentioned that the *Titanic* still had workmen onboard when she sailed on her maiden voyage. In my experience, there is nothing unusual for a few technicians and workmen to sail on a ship for it's first voyage as there are usually several minor problems to iron out once the vessel enters service. It's well known that each night when most onboard of the *Titanic* were asleep in their cabins, one or two Harland and Wolff technicians would be called on, to carry out further inspections and calculations for improvements in the first and second class public rooms. Much of the ship's decor and fittings were an improvement on her sister ship the *Olympic,* but White Star Line were determined that the *Titanic* would be the best vessel the company had built to date and the slightest flaw in design or comfort would go under the microscope during the voyage. This work would be carried out in the dead of night to prevent any inconvenience to passengers during the daylight hours.

The crew would have had most of their accommodation at the forward end of the ship and apart from having their food catered for by the shipping company, White Star Line would have provided little else. Most of their clothing, bedding and washing facilities they would have had to find for themselves and even back in the fifties when I first went to sea, I still had to supply my own towel. Maritime unions were beginning to have some impact on ship owners in those days regarding the welfare of seafarers at sea, but their living conditions even on such a fine ship as the *Titanic,* still left much to be desired. On the dockside in those days it was a common sight for crew joining a ship to buy a straw mattress for something like two shillings, known commonly as a 'donkey's feed bag.'

I would tell the public that quite a few of the seamen that had sailed on the ship, were ex Royal Navy personnel and were experienced seafarers although it was a known fact that most of the catering staff, despite being at sea for many years, would have little knowledge of basic seamanship.

Fifth Officer Lowe, the officer in charge of Lifeboat 14, had never travelled across the Atlantic before and knew none of the crew including his fellow officers. This voyage was a new experience for him and later on, his knowledge of seamanship and leadership qualities would be put to the ultimate test. Lookout men would receive 5 pounds a month wages, the same as other Able Seamen, although they would receive an extra 5 shillings a month for carrying out their lookout duties. It's interesting to note that when I did the same job as Lookout Man some 45 years later on the Cunard White Star liners across the North Atlantic, I received just two pounds a month extra for my duties in the crows nest.

As the *Titanic* steamed through the night, there would be a few night stewards on duty, setting up dining room tables in the dining saloons for breakfast the following morning along with night bakers turning out bread and hundreds of bread rolls. A Night Pantry man would be on duty for the first and second class, to answer the call of any passengers requiring a snack during the night. He would also prepare coffee and sandwiches for the officers of the watch, which would be taken up to them by a junior seaman known as a Bridge Boy. The *Titanic* was a floating city and as her passengers slept, much would be quietly going on throughout the night to ensure maximum comfort and service each day whilst onboard this wonderful ship.

There were many questions about the actual building of the *Titanic* and the inferior steel used in her construction. I'm certainly no naval architect but I have reason to believe that the materials used in the building of that ship was the best available at that time. This probably came about by scientific tests carried out by Americans after bringing up pieces of steel from the wreck site and revealing that the metal was porous and below standard. It probably was on today's standards but they didn't have the same technology then as they do today and besides, the Royal Navy was built with the same type of steel in those days as was the *Olympic* and she completed over 500 voyages across the Atlantic before being scrapped some 28 years later.

This criticism of the ship's steel was another attempt by some to discredit the *Titanic* in its entirety and probably because the vessel broke in half during her final plunge to the bottom of the ocean. The steel would have been close to freezing point and not being a metallurgist, I would imagine a bit more brittle than it may otherwise have been. When a ship of that size is sinking by the bow and the stern continues to rise ever higher out of the water, lifting with it several thousand tons of machinery and coal, something eventually will give. The ship had two expansion plates on the upper decks, one between the first and second funnel and the other between the third and fourth funnel and these would have been weak points, exacerbating the problem. Eventually, the ship did break across the expansion plate between the third and fourth funnel.

Another criticism was the apparently small rudder on the *Titanic* but this again came from those trying to make the story even more scandalous than that already achieved by storytellers and filmmakers everywhere. It was claimed that with such a small rudder, the ship would be slow in answering her helm but with a larger rudder, may well have swung just enough to clear the iceberg. The *Titanic* had three propellers and the one in the centre would be thrusting water onto the rudder giving the vessel ample steerageway when at sea, and she would have answered her helm positively, after striking the iceberg when the wheel was ordered to go 'hard to port.' It's a pity that all three engines were stopped as putting the port engine at full astern may well have helped her round quicker, to avoid damage to the bow section.

Unfortunately, a collision would have still been inevitable as she may well have struck the iceberg around the mid ships section or half way along, perhaps causing more damage and resulting in the ship sinking even quicker. For a ship of that size to steer around that iceberg, they would have needed more time but the iceberg was upon them before they could do much about it. Engine room movements may well have assisted the manoeuvre but again the response would have been slow and again, more time was needed. There were many theories from the public on what should have been done and what shouldn't have happened but these comments of mine, which I feel are of a common sense nature, would usually satisfy most of the critics.

I would like to point out that I have used modern day terminology when referring to the port and starboard sides of the ship whereas in 1912, it was the opposite.

My only criticism of that episode is that in an ice routine situation, the engine room should have been put on standby that night and to date, I've never read anything to suggest that it was, in which case it would have given all concerned a quicker response to their predicament. Had the engine room been on standby, then the watertight doors would have also been shut which was common ice routine procedure when I was at sea in those regions, although we now know they were of no use after the serious collision with the iceberg anyway. However, hindsight is something else and without doubt, that iceberg had their name on it.

During my several lectures on the *Titanic*, I would try to give the public an insight into the reasons behind the building of the great White Star liners and the lucrative mail contracts involved with the North Atlantic carriers. Many of the public would show surprise when I explained the mail contract and how the White Star Line had the edge on the rest. Operators on that trade carrying mails to America, would unload on the dock side and then the mail would go to the sorting houses before going on their various journeys across the United States. With the *Titanic*, she would have her own mail sorters onboard sorting mail on a 12 hours shift throughout the voyage and on arrival in New York, mail was already sorted, bagged up and ready for despatch to the various states. This would save days on the delivery of mail and no other shipping companies could compete with White Star along those lines.

The carrying of emigrants across to America was increasing all the time and once settled in their new land, they would write letters home and inspire others to follow suit which meant that White Star would carry them and their mail backwards and forwards on an ever increasing trade, this being the ship owner's dream. The *Titanic* and ships like her were part of that dream but there were lessons to be learned and history has told us that there was a price to pay. As a result, shipping companies world wide were to learn from the *Titanic* experience and ocean going liners are now perhaps one of the safest modes of transport in the world.

Towards the end of June, the Exhibition at South Bank was drawing to a close and on Monday July 5, closed its doors after nine weeks in the city. Before closing their doors for the last time in Brisbane, I was asked by the management of the exhibition, if I would consider rejoining them again when they reopen in Auckland in New Zealand in September. This would be for five weeks and then on to Wellington thereafter. I took them up on their offer and flew out there for their opening on September 18 at the Aotea Centre in the city of Auckland.

The exhibition turned out to be smaller than the original plan due to the restriction on space but it still generated a considerable amount of interest. My appearance on the very popular, 'Holmes' public affairs, television program in Auckland, created quite a bit of interest for the exhibition. As a result, many enthusiasts turned up due to that showing. Among those attending, were two separate families that introduced themselves to me at the exhibition with the same name as mine. We came to the same conclusion as regards to the origin of our fairly unusual family name, which still remains a bit of a mystery.

As in Brisbane, the interest by the public, far outweighed the business of just selling books and as always, I was telling them a story, which for me, was a labour of love anyway.

Perhaps, some of the most surprising observations at the exhibition in Auckland as in Brisbane were by school children, asking the most extraordinary questions. One young chap no more than around nine years of age, stood in front of my table and introduced himself, offering out his hand for a hand shake. After I shook his hand he went on, ' may I ask you some questions on the *Titanic* Mr Haisman?' ' Certainly ' I replied as he went on in depth asking question after question on the ship's construction, speed and horsepower, finally asking if my mother had suffered in any way. At the end of the questioning, he once again thanked me for my time and shook hands once more before leaving to rejoin his parents. They no doubt had plans of turning this young fellow into a gentleman.

At the exhibition, there were two beautiful scale models of the *Titanic* lying on the seabed, as she would appear today. The bow section was in one glass cabinet and some distance away, the stern section, also in a glass cabinet, representing the ship as it lies on the ocean floor. A young girl, about ten years of age, came up to my table and said, ' excuse me. Did you know that your models are the wrong way round?' It wasn't up to me to organise any of the displays and quite frankly I hadn't taken much notice of the models anyway, but closer scrutiny revealed that she was absolutely right, the stern section was facing the wrong way!

For the five weeks that the exhibition was in Auckland it had been fairly successful but not enough according to the organisers who decided to cancel moving on to Wellington. During this time I had been invited out to dinner on the occasion and I found the New Zealanders a friendly bunch and very British in many ways. For me, both exhibitions had been quite an experience, meeting such a wide range of people, listening to their many questions and their opinions on all things *Titanic*. The exhibition closed on October 24 and I flew back to Brisbane the next day having no idea where the exhibition would go after this venue, although Melbourne had been hinted at several times.

In December of 1999, my wife and I flew back to England for the millennium celebrations to be with our remaining families and friends for this special time in all our lives. It was great fun to be having a beer again with Bob and Froggy and as usual, we were like three kids again, with our reminiscences. Froggy now sports a beard and apart from that, is much the same, still retaining that boyish sense of humour and is employed as a Club Bosun at a sailing club on the Hamble River. Bob has never changed either, remaining generous to a fault with a complete ' couldn't care less', attitude and now retired, passes his time away as a bingo fanatic, always looking for ' the big one.'

On returning to Brisbane in January 2000, my sister and I, along with my wife Lyn, were invited to attend the opening of the *Titanic* Bar at the Tugun Tavern down at the Gold Coast. It was a well, organised evening and a lot of fun and should anyone venture down there they will find several items of interest regarding the *Titanic* story including one of my paintings.

On May 15, 2000, I briefly addressed some 1 200 boys at St Laurences College during morning assembly, talking about my mother's involvement with the *Titanic* and presenting the school with a copy of my book and a poster of one of my paintings. It remains extraordinary the interest still shown by many people in all walks of life and more particularly, the young.

Looking back over the past century, I feel extremely privileged to have been around at that time with the many inventions that have had such an effect on our lives. When my parents were born towards the end of the last century, people had never heard about such things as electricity, motorcars, radio, air travel, televisions, movies, computers, or even space travel. Today, these things are taken for granted and are part of our rich tapestry of life and we continue to look for even more things to improve our life styles. Clearly, mankind will continue to make strides forward at a greater pace, now with the help of computers, leaving people like me, finding it impossible to imagine what life will be like at the end of the next century. With the last century came the disasters, many of these disasters due to mankind's complacency when dealing with nature. The violence of hurricanes, tornados, cyclones and flooding, never cease to amaze us with their intensity and although much wiser these days, we still get ' caught out ' by the elements.

The *Titanic* disaster was one of the worst shipping disasters of the last century and this was brought about by a chain of events leading up to a complete disregard for the forces of nature. There was no violent storm or heavy sea on April 15, 1912, just one huge solitary iceberg, drifting silently with the currents into the path of the *Titanic*. On a flat calm sea, during a bitterly cold, star studded, moonless night in the North Atlantic, Mother Nature took the lives of over 1500 souls.

She was to deal an efficient, lethal blow, leaving mankind once again 'caught out ', as the iceberg continued to drift south, getting smaller each day until finally, becoming part of the sea, all the evidence completely, efficiently, destroyed. We had all been taught another bitter lesson by the unpredictable forces of nature.

Looking back to the time of my birth in England during early April of 1938, the government of the day announced that all Britons would be measured for gas masks. The U.K. police, recommended that all bicycles should have a red rear lamp and the top rate of income tax was five shillings and sixpence, (about A64 cents) On my birthday, April 28, a government committee announced that all workers should have one week's paid holiday as an entitlement.

Today there are plans to make further dives on the *Titanic* wreck site to retrieve more artefacts, this time with remote controlled submersibles, which will explore even further into the wreck. Perhaps the *Titanic* has generated more money as a wreck, than she would ever have done if she had completed her normal sea going career of some 30 years. Finally, there has been news from time to time, revealing that a replica of the *Titanic* will be built and she will complete that voyage across the North Atlantic from Southampton to New York. I shall look forward to that.

> *Living with Titanic throughout the years,*
> *has brought home the drama, tragedy and*
> *tears.*
> *The continuing dives on the wreck should*
> *cease,*
> *Allowing the Titanic to rest in peace.*

Haisey.

THE END

EPILOGUE

WHEN DECIDING to write my autobiography, it was put to me that another *Titanic* story would go down like a lead balloon and I agreed with that – up to a point. I suspect timing is the ultimate in many stories, along with content and perhaps the end of the millenium is as good a time as any to get out there with one's scribblings.

So how do you go about writing a life story when so much of that life has been involved with the sea and one has been raised on the story of one of the world's greatest shipping disasters? It would be difficult to entirely disregard that tragedy and besides, it was because of that disaster that I am here today. However, this saga will return at specific anniversaries, the next being in April 2002, ninety years since the disaster. It has been rumoured that another *Titanic* will be built to mark that anniversary and in the light of that I can only hope that I have a story that is connected, but with a difference, revealing some facts and bringing a freshness to a well-flogged story.

I have always enjoyed belonging to a big family, but being the youngest has seen the disadvantages of having little in common with my older brothers and sisters, due to the age gap. My eldest brother, for instance, was twenty years older than me and as a result I barely knew the man.

My own generation has, since its inception back in 1918, has had its fair share of tragedy with the deaths of three children – Brian, David and Steven – and my mother enduring the grief of outliving four of her ten children as well as her husband.. No parent wants to outlive her offspring, but perhaps this is one of the drawbacks of living to be one hundred years of age.

It's been said that a rolling stone gathers no moss and I suppose that may well be a fitting description of my own life. But the travel has been fun, and priceless, and I still can't get enough of it, even today. As long as this is the case I shall continue to feel alive; and long may it last!

This, then, in the first years of a new millenium, is my story to date and the way I see it. Perhaps the six surviving members of my family may see things differently, but that would be their story.

Haisey.